Advanced Praise for *Embracing the Mixed Ecology*

"Dwight Zscheile and Blair Pogue are two of the brightest minds in Episcopal theology and practice. With *Embracing the Mixed Ecology*, they come together to deftly analyze our changing church and changing world, and then offer illuminating pictures of ministries shaped for the future. This wonderful book will make you think *and* make you hope."

—Stephanie Spellers, Episcopal priest and author of *The Church Cracked Open* and *Radical Welcome*

"A thoughtful and challenging book that approaches the crisis in the church today with a clear-eyed and commonsensical view of what is needed and what lies before us as we seek, as a Christian community, to act as God's hands in the world. The church, as the authors beautifully explain, both embodies and enacts encounters with the risen Christ. This seems especially relevant now, as we confront a world fractured along tribal and political lines. I strongly recommend this book."

—Jay Parini, author of *Jesus: The Human Face of God* and New York Times bestselling author of *The Last Station*

"This book will change how you think about church, and... open your eyes to see how and where God is at work in the corners of our communities, among ordinary people, in unexpected and extraordinary ways. With uncommon wisdom and a spirit of generosity, Zscheile and Pogue invite us on a journey of transformation, into a future with hope."

—Louise N. Johnson, Executive for Vision, Evangelical Lutheran Church in America

"The 'mixed ecology' metaphor is so helpful for understanding the re-shaping of our churches for mission.... Zscheile and Pogue explore the many rich forms this metaphor takes as it lands across various church movements... Read the book and take the journey every pastor, leader, and Christian must take in these challenging times."

—David Fitch, author of *Faithful Presence*

"With a Christological lens and a generous spirit, Zscheile and Pogue have created a faithful and imagination-widening book for ecclesial leaders."

—Nick Warnes, Executive Director, Cyclical INC

"A really excellent survey of the field—easy to read, balanced, carefully researched, wide ranging, and with lots of inspiring stories. It deserves to be widely read."

—Dr. Michael Moynagh, author, advocate,
theologian and consultant on new Christian communities

"[A] wonderful overview of the diversity of the mixed ecology. A must read for all church leaders!"

—Ed Olsworth-Peter,
Director of Innovation, St. Mellitus College

"A perceptive and illuminating analysis of why a mixed ecology of church is so vital in our contemporary cultural context in the West."

—Mike Harrison, Bishop of Exeter, United Kingdom

"In an age when Christendom's project to hold the center of social and cultural influence has reached a decisive end, this book offers an extraordinarily simple and compelling invitation to return to our core work of following Jesus as a way of life."

—Craig Loya,
Bishop of The Episcopal Church in Minnesota

EMBRACING THE MIXED ECOLOGY

Inherited and New Forms of Christian Community Flourishing Together

DWIGHT J. ZSCHEILE
BLAIR A. POGUE

Seabury Books
NEW YORK

Seabury Books
19 East 34th Street
New York, NY 10016
www.churchpublishing.org

Seabury Books is an imprint of Church Publishing Incorporated

Cover design by Newgen
Typeset by Nord Compo

ISBN 978-1-64065-771-7 (paperback)
ISBN 978-1-64065-770-0 (hardback)
ISBN 978-1-64065-772-4 (eBook)

Library of Congress Control Number: 2024947736

For all the people Jesus loves
who don't participate in church.

Table of Contents

Acknowledgments

This book is the product of our research, experience, and explorations at the local, regional, national, and international levels over the past several years. We're deeply grateful for the many people who have contributed to our learning and the many partners with whom we have walked. These include Dawn Alitz, Jon Anderson, Michael Beck, Michael Binder, Susan Brooks, Terri Elton, Alicia Granholm, Rolf Jacobson, Katie Langston, Bishop Craig Loya, Jeckonia Okoth, Karen Olson, Tessa Pinkstaff, Grace Pomroy, Kelsey Schuster, Sean Steele, Robin Steinke, and Steve Thomason. We are also grateful to the institutions where we work that have supported this work, Luther Seminary and the Episcopal Church in Minnesota.

We have been blessed by several visits to the UK in the past five years, where the church's negotiation of a post-Christian society has been deeply illuminating. Among our conversation partners and hosts have been Bishop Mike Harrison (whose extraordinary hospitality we're very grateful for), Michael Moynagh, Ed Olsworth-Peter, Sally Gaze, Nick Shepherd, John McGinley, Harvey Kwiyani, Jonny Baker, Cathy Ross, Chigor Chike, Wole Agbaje, Alix Taylor, Diane Grano, Fiona Mayne, and Jason Fout. The Lightwave Community of pioneer leaders in the Suffolk area generously shared their stories and learnings with us.

We're deeply thankful for the friends and colleagues who took the time to read the manuscript and offer constructive feedback: Jon Anderson, Kathy Brekken, Susan Brooks, Nicole Bullock, Sally Gaze, David Hayes, Drew and Tina Hofler, Milan Homola, F. Willis Johnson, Gary Johnson, Harvey Kwiyani, Terese Lewis, Dave Male, Michael Moynagh, Ed Olsworth-Peter, Tessa Pinkstaff, Grace Pomroy, Stephanie Spellers, Sean Steele, Robin Steinke, Nick Warnes, Bill Withers, and JR Woodward.

Introduction

When we arrived at St. Matthew's Episcopal Church in St. Paul, Minnesota 20 years ago, this neighborhood church tucked away on a side street was both struggling and full of promise. Founded in 1889, with its current building constructed in 1914, St. Matthew's reflected the academic orientation of its neighborhood near a state university campus, with a theologically broad and intellectually inquisitive ethos. Over the years, it had learned how to lean outward in service to neighbors by offering meals, housing unsheltered families in its space, and helping start and support an orphanage in Uganda. Like many congregations, the people of the church loved each other. One member said that if her house burned down, all she would need is the church directory, because she knew the congregation would surround her and provide what she and her family needed.

St. Matthew's was rather unique in having a significant number of global majority members,[1] many of whom initially came to the United States to study at the nearby university. They represented a dozen different nations, primarily from Africa. Their presence changed and deepened the spirituality of the church. One of those leaders, Beatrice Garubanda, started a ministry with African immigrant children. St. Matthew's members still recount the story of the time a young man who grew up in the church was involved in an accident in Belize. He was underwater long enough to be brain dead. His mother called the church asking for prayers. Beatrice stopped everyone in the parish hall in the midst of their coffee hour conversations and prayed a prayer in which God's power and presence were felt palpably. The young man survived.

Yet, like so many older churches, St. Matthew's also struggled. It almost closed its doors in the 1980s after a fire in the sanctuary on Easter Day. Most members had a hard time articulating the difference their Christian faith made to their lives. During more than 16 years serving this congregation as clergy, we embarked upon a number of experiments and initiatives to deepen the church's connections to God, other church members, and their neighbors. This included the development of a vision for the Christian life that we called the Way of Jesus, the introduction of simple practices of imaginatively listening to scripture in community, the cultivation of spaces of storytelling about how God was at work in people's lives, and the creation of groups around different vocations where people could reflect on how God might be calling them to follow Jesus as educators, healthcare workers, social workers, and business people.[2] We collaborated with global majority members to incorporate liturgies, music, art, practices, and food from their cultures more deeply into the life of the church.

Although St. Matthew's was spiritually vital and full of engaging offerings, including global worship, an experimental and more participatory Sunday evening service, a wide range of adult education topics, impactful outreach ministries, and lots of opportunities for communal meals and fellowship, these offerings were not of interest to most of the church's neighbors. When interviewed, neighbors mentioned that they were looking for community and "safe places" like the local library where there was "no agenda." Occasionally a neighborhood couple or two would come to an adult faith forum for a "meaning of life" topic, but the church's more formal, liturgical worship was not widely appealing, and its Christian faith was suspect in a left-leaning neighborhood. During COVID-19, the church took its worship outdoors into a park across the street. This allowed not only for greater safety in gathering during a pandemic, but also opportunities for more visibility with neighbors walking their dogs. Yet, like many churches, the congregation wasn't ready or particularly interested in going deeper in listening to these neighbors, meeting them where they were in spaces that were comfortable to them, and adapting its life in order to form Christian community with them.

We share this story because we love traditional local churches like St. Matthew's and have been deeply formed in and by them. We have served them for much of our lives. They are communities in which people come to know the power of the gospel of Jesus, experience the grace of Christian community, and are equipped for ministry. They are places where God knits people together for love and service. At their best, they are a sign, witness, instrument, and foretaste of God's kingdom or reign.[3] There is beauty and power in their life and witness.

We also know they are not connecting with increasing numbers of people in their contexts, like St. Matthew's neighbors. We know this first of all on a very personal level: we both grew up outside the church in secular homes in California. We were formed in the dominant narratives of late modern Western culture, which place the autonomous individual self as the ultimate authority, assume one can live a good life without God, reduce faith and spirituality to matters of private preference, and either construe history as a trajectory of technological progress toward some future optimization or pessimistically see it as a power struggle between identity groups with no just resolution. Neither of us knew much about traditional churches, what took place inside them, or what they might offer to our yearnings for identity, belonging, meaning, and purpose. If we had taken the risk to show up in those churches, what we found there would have been largely culturally inaccessible to us.

We were fortunate. A couple of Christians found us where we were, embodied God's grace and love, and translated the gospel of Jesus's healing of the whole of life into terms we could understand. Our own journeys have taken us through parachurch student and campus ministries, traditional churches, church plants, and a variety of expressions of Christian community and ministry. We have experienced the richness of both mainline and evangelical Protestantism as well as their limitations, frustrations, and failings. We are writing this book because we don't take the gospel of Jesus for granted. For both of us, it is a matter of life and death, an alternative and countercultural story that is so much more life-giving than the dominant culture's narratives. Our lives and ministries have been dedicated to serving that gospel and helping churches deepen their life in it as well as their connections with neighbors, for we know what it is like to live without Christ. We also know how hard it is for churches to connect meaningfully with their neighbors today.

A Time of Disconnection

We live in an age of disconnection in America and other Western societies, even as we are more technologically connected. This disconnection is unfolding on multiple fronts. Technology has accelerated the formation of polarized cultural tribes, separating us from one another across ethnic, political, socioeconomic, and religious lines. Despite real historical progress, longstanding racial divisions persist and are easily inflamed in an era of scapegoating and conflict entrepreneurship.[4] Prevailing cultural narratives place identity as the central marker of human life in ways that suggest our experiences are incommensurable and mutually incomprehensible. At this moment, there is a lot of money and power to be gained in fomenting resentment, division, hate, and estrangement.

Increasing numbers of people are also disconnected from institutions generally and religious institutions specifically. As we explore in chapter 1, there is a massive generational disengagement from affiliation and participation in religious organizations and voluntary associations of all kinds in Western societies. There are complex reasons for this, which we unpack later, but the result is an increasingly go-it-alone approach to faith and spirituality, even as many people crave to experience deep belonging in authentic community.

This disengagement from religious institutions isn't just for the so-called "nones"—the people who profess no religious affiliation. It is also increasingly a phenomenon among the "dones"—those who have left church or other religious institutions.[5] Many of these people still consider themselves faithful Christians even though they cannot find a Christian community they find hospitable and trustworthy. Some of the most faithful Christian disciples we know are no longer connected to institutional expressions of church. Some have had painful experiences of spiritual harm. Others work on Sundays or participate in activities where they find more community and meaning than in organized church. Some look in vain for vital expressions of Christian community that will help them follow Jesus faithfully in culturally accessible, grounded ways. Many of our inherited church institutions are failing to do this.

This book explores the forms of Christian community and witness that can faithfully thrive in today's world. There is no one answer to that question, but rather a multiplicity, reflecting the complexity of the missionary environment in which the church finds itself. It is not a matter of rejecting legacy forms of institutional church outright, as some might be tempted to do. Nor is it a matter of chasing the latest fad or model that will provide a quick fix. There are no quick fixes. The premise of a quick fix is itself a modern Western cultural narrative, grounded in the assumption that human agency and technology can save us. This moment calls for a different kind of imagination, posture, and practice than the dominant forms that churches have maintained in recent decades, and that the dominant culture provides.

We want to state at the outset that we are not romantics about inventing or discovering a post-institutional church that functions as pure movement without any of the complexities of institutional life. Some form of institutional life is necessary for any movement to survive and pass its life on over time.

We treasure the riches of the Christian tradition and don't want to see them abandoned. Institutions are vessels for their preservation across generations. Humans are sinful as well as holy beings, and order and accountability are required to safeguard a community's life. In a time of disconnection, the solution is neither idealistically abandoning nor doubling down on particular inherited structures, but rather recovering fresh *imagination* from scripture and the Christian tradition for how Christian community might be embodied for faithful witness in a changing world. Along with this imagination comes a particular *posture*—of humility, listening, and experimentation—that is embodied in *practices* that may seem strange for many inherited churches. This shift in imagination, posture, and practice is the focus of this book.

The Mixed Ecology

Scripture is full of ecological imagery. Genesis 2 describes God creating the world as a vibrant garden with humanity embedded within it. The Mosaic law includes discussion of farming, food production, and feasting with an eye toward generosity and justice. The prophetic literature uses the metaphor of a vineyard to describe the relationship between God and God's people. In Jeremiah 29, God dictates to the exiles in Babylon a message of encouragement to plant gardens and put down roots even amidst their trauma, loss, and displacement.

Jesus picks up this long tradition and builds upon it in his teachings. The word of God is like seed scattered by a sower, with varying degrees of fruitfulness (Mark 4). Toward the end of his ministry with his disciples, Jesus describes himself as the vine and his followers as branches (John 15). Paul talks about planting, watering, and God giving the growth (1 Corinthians 3:6). Long before modern industrial farming, food production, and climate control, people in biblical contexts were intimately familiar with the beauty and fragility of ecological growth. This wasn't just a gardening hobby; it was a matter of survival.

What the church needs today is a *mixed ecology* of inherited and new forms of Christian community working together for the sake of faithful witness. Imagine a garden with many different types of plants and trees flourishing alongside one another. They share sunlight, water, soil, shade, and nutrients. Through their interconnections and proximity, they support a richer array of life than any one species alone could offer. The mixed ecology is the church version of this garden, where multiple forms of Christian community coexist and mutually support one another for the sake of loving and witnessing to the diversity of people, generations, and cultures present in a particular environment.

The concept of a mixed ecology emerged within the UK over the past few decades as a way to describe both the value and importance of longstanding institutional church structures (which in that context could be well over 1,000 years old) alongside new forms of Christian community that connect more readily with people in today's world.[6] The Church of England remains the state or established church even as Christian practice and participation have dropped below 10 percent of the population.[7] As we explore in an extended case study later, this has led to both a reckoning on the state of the church's vitality and witness and permission and support for many creative expressions of church. These all belong together. As Ric Thorpe, bishop for church planting in the Church of England, likes to say, "We need everything to reach everyone."[8]

The word "inherited" invokes the multiple dimensions of an inheritance. It is not earned or achieved, but received as a gift from previous generations. Inheritances are valuable. They can also be complicated, bequeathing things that may not always fit well within the lives of succeeding generations. Think about how many millennials want their parents' antiques, for example! When we use the terms "new" or "innovative," we also want to be careful. Many of the most fruitful forms of community life and practice that are emerging today are retrievals of ancient forms that had been abandoned or forgotten. They may be familiar in some traditions of the church but seem new to others.

We find Peter J. Denning and Robert Dunham's definition of innovation as "the adoption of a new practice in a community" to be most helpful.[9] The category of innovation is unfruitful if it invokes a kind of late-modern technological quest for the latest institutional fix based on human agency (rather than divine presence, agency, and leadership). When we use the term "innovation" in this book, we hope to undercut such late modern technical conceptualizations. Innovative forms of church faithfully adapt Christian identity, practice, and witness in changing cultural contexts, but primarily through prayer, presence, and humble experimentation as we seek to follow God's leading. This is what the church has always done throughout the ages in differing times and places. We explore this more deeply in chapter 2.

The mixed ecology is a *both/and*. It affirms the deep richness of the past and the faithful ways Christians have passed on the church's life over the ages. At the same time, it recognizes that we are in a new cultural moment that calls for fresh discernment of God's leading. Steve Aisthorpe uses the metaphor "rewilding" to describe what is required now. He points out that our late-modern appetite to plan, manage, contain, and control has disrupted natural patterns of growth and development in the life of the church.[10] Within the world of ecology, "rewilding" means restoring an area of land to its natural uncultivated state, thereby permitting ecological processes to resume. For the churches in Western culture who are inheritors both of the legacy of Christendom (when the church was culturally and socially privileged) and modernity, which eclipses God's agency in favor of human agency, rewilding is a paradigm shift. As Aisthorpe describes: "Rewilding the church is not about implementing our best ideas with unusual passion; it requires stopping or slowing down, a conscious setting aside of preconceptions and a determination to discern what God is doing and our role in that."[11]

Learning to Inhabit the Margins

Christianity in Western societies bears a particularly complicated legacy of having once been a privileged majority faith. Beginning with the Roman emperor Constantine in the early 4th century, Christianity came to occupy a central role in society in the

West. Over time, Christianity became a territorial and tribal faith coextensive to a large degree with European civilization itself. This was the ideal of "Christendom." The church benefited significantly from this arrangement, ceasing to be a persecuted community struggling for survival and becoming a primary cultural influence. Western culture benefited from Christianity being normalized, as values such as mercy, greater equality among persons, forgiveness rather than vengeance, human rights, and service on behalf of the common good became more widespread.[12] At the same time, the church's identity as a minority movement within a hostile, pagan culture profoundly changed. Power and privilege, political and military entanglement, clericalism, elitism, and imperialism all reshaped the church's life and witness.[13]

While this is not the place to explore that legacy in detail, it is critical to recognize that the era of Christendom has largely come to an end in Western societies. The societies in Europe that have state churches are more advanced in their rejection of Christian faith and practice. The United States, with its free market religious economy and high levels of immigration, is also experiencing this shift, though a generation behind. Yet, within white communities at least, American churches on all sides of the political and theological spectrum still tend to assume they can remake the nation in their image. Enormous energy is still being spent on evangelistic, missionary, and advocacy efforts undergirded by Christendom assumptions.

For instance, the church growth movement that emerged in the 1970s and 80s primarily focused on attracting people to worship services. This worked (and in some places still works) with people who have a Christian background and who are looking for a church to join. Much of the growth in evangelical, Pentecostal, and some mainline churches during the last few decades of the 20th century was "switching"—the affiliation of disaffiliated (often mainline and Roman Catholic) believers into other congregations that were more culturally accessible and vibrant. Stronger and newer churches gained more of the population from less vibrant and less accessible traditional churches. However, all of this assumes a basic familiarity with Christianity, that unaffiliated people are seeking a church to join, and that worship is the primary place of connection for these neighbors. Don't get us wrong—we think it is great when people who are disconnected from participation in church find a vital church to join. But as our Christian siblings in Europe have discovered, church growth is not the solution to a culture that is increasingly hostile to, unfamiliar with, or rejecting Christian faith.

Another version of this is the concept of "revival." Revivals have often emerged in places where the institutional church has been culturally and socially established for some time but has fallen into spiritual lethargy, cultural inaccessibility, and irrelevance. The evangelical movement itself emerged in Europe in the 18th and 19th centuries as a means to reanimate dormant faith within the basic paradigm of Christendom. Churches that had grown anemic in their spiritual vitality and ability to help people know God and follow Jesus experienced revival movements such as pietism, Methodism, and the Great Awakenings, which challenged them to reform. Revival is one way in which the Spirit of God renews the church. Like church growth, we think revival is wonderful when it reignites faith, commitment, and purpose. Yet the assumption of revivals tends to be that people have a latent Christian faith to reanimate. That is less and less the case in Western societies today.[14]

Political and social advocacy is another way in which churches can operate from a Christendom mindset. Denominations or other church bodies make social statements and pronouncements on various political issues with the assumption that they have moral credibility and will influence the nation. These statements and pronouncements are generally ignored by the wider public and policymakers alike. The rise of the Religious Right in America in the later decades of the 20th century was another Christendom response to a secularizing and pluralizing nation. While public witness is a legitimate part of Christian mission, assuming the church can speak from a place of cultural privilege today is misguided. Trying to coercively impose a particular Christian political vision on a pluralist society will only backfire among those already skeptical of the church. Writing from the UK context, Stuart Murray suggests the church today should learn to live as a "prophetic minority."[15]

For mainline Protestant denominations in the United States that are inheritors of the European state churches, the logic of Christendom is deeply embedded in their DNA and difficult to unlearn. They have long seen themselves as standing at the center of their communities and society. The Washington National Cathedral, for instance, is a prominent artifact of this ethos. Conservative evangelical churches that embrace political activism in order to create their own version of a Christian America can fall prey to their own form of nationalist idolatry.[16]

For all of these churches, a lot of unlearning and new learning will be required. Dutch scholar Stefan Paas writes, "Only if we become weak, will people be prepared to listen. Only if people do not feel threatened by an institutional grasp for power by Christians will they feel free to appreciate what Christians have to tell."[17]

Unlearning the assumptions of Christendom will involve a spiritual journey of dispossession, self-examination, prayer, and humility as churches in the dominant culture shift from a "come to us on our terms" posture to joining neighbors where they are, by first listening, then loving, and serving. The narratives of cultural and social privilege need to be challenged by the biblical narrative. The church's credibility, especially with younger generations, has eroded dramatically. Trust will only be regained through patient, local practice in relationships where we listen and love first.

Of course, the Black church, immigrant churches, and other minority ethnic churches in Western societies have long inhabited the space, posture, and practices of being a prophetic minority on the margins. Their marginality has often allowed them to retain and offer a more holistic witness to the gospel than the dominant-culture churches of Christendom. While those traditions have their own challenges at this moment, they tend to be less co-opted by the cultural narratives of Enlightenment modernity. God's power, presence, and agency are palpable in communities that don't have the illusion of being in control of the world. The biblical identity of God's people as a suffering community and God as a God of justice who joins us in our suffering in Christ to redeem and restore human life strongly resonates.

The presence of global majority heritage Christians in the midst of Western societies is growing significantly through migration. With the exponential growth of the church in Africa, Asia, and Latin America, Christianity is now primarily a religion of the Global South, not the West.[18] Harvey Kwiyani observes:

> In the United States, just as in Europe, hundreds of African immigrant churches have sprung up in the past 20 years. Most of them are conservative and charismatic in their theology. They do not employ the spiritual/material dichotomy seen in most of Western Christianity. As they become more visible on the Western Christian landscape, they will slowly become more identified with Christianity itself.[19]

The Holy Spirit is offering many gifts and opportunities for mutual learning, exchange, and renewal through intercultural encounters within and across churches. In the 21st century, mission is likely to flow not from the "the West to the rest" as in the colonial era, but from "the rest to the West" through migration. Peter Vethanayagamony observes that this involves mission from the global poor and marginalized to the rich and powerful, which is how the original apostolic movement of Christianity started among Galilean Jews amidst the Roman Empire.[20]

Throughout this book, we trace some of the dimensions of unlearning and new learning that the shift toward being a prophetic minority involves for churches used to being at the cultural and social center. At its heart, it means rediscovering the centrality, power, and simplicity of following Jesus as disciples in the power of the Holy Spirit amidst competing narratives, practices, and formative influences. Christian witness from on high in the form of big institutional schemes, programs, or pronouncements will be far less faithful and effective today than local teams of disciples organically *being with* their neighbors in love, listening with openness to their questions and doubts, compassionately working for healing, justice, and peace, and gently but boldly inviting people to discover the power of life in Christ as an alternative way.[21] Jehu Hanciles describes this as "witness as withness" in his study of African immigrant missions in the West.[22]

This work of cultivating discipleship as an alternative way of life and love and evangelism/mission as joining neighbors in community spaces to accompany and love them in the name of Jesus is important. It's also not what many inherited churches are focused on or designed for. It requires new spaces, practices, and habits, all of which must be discerned prayerfully. There are many ways in which the church will be tempted in this moment of disruption and disintegration to adopt cultural norms that can lead it astray.

The Mixed Ecology Is Nothing New

The good news is that when we step back and take a longer view, the church has embodied many different forms throughout its history, often simultaneously. Within the Bible itself, the Jewish community made the transition from a people wandering the wilderness with the ark of the covenant to a people focused on the Jerusalem Temple as the center of their religious life. This was then destroyed not once, but twice. Synagogues and domestic worship became the primary alternative ways to organize Jewish religious life.

This is the milieu in which the Christian church emerged as a movement of Jewish followers of a Jewish rabbi, Jesus. Christianity embraced house churches before eventually adopting other community spaces such as basilicas, which were Roman civic gathering spaces. The early Christians chose the word *ekklesia* (Greek for "public assembly") to describe themselves in contrast to the private cults that were common in pagan society at the time. The church was first and foremost a *community of people* gathered around experiences and stories of the risen Christ in the power of the Spirit. We explore in chapter 2 some of the various forms of Christian community and witness that have coexisted alongside established or predominant ways of being church in various contexts. There is much in the church's own history to retrieve and reclaim for this moment.

As we take this journey in the following chapters, we invite you to bring a posture of curiosity about some of the ways Christian community life is being formed and embodied today in different contexts. Some of the examples we share and the stories we tell may not resonate with you, either theologically, culturally, or in terms of your own ecclesiology, piety, and practice. We have deliberately chosen an ecumenical breadth of case stories and models. Not all of them will work in all places or with all people.

That is the point of a mixed ecology—diversity is necessary to reach a diverse society and world. We try to highlight both risks and possibilities in each of these approaches, and to reflect critically on them. There is no one solution, no one size or shape to fit all. We have drawn many of our case studies from the UK, where the mixed ecology has been intentionally developed over the past few decades. The church's post-Christian context there is farther advanced and gives insights into America's future if current trends hold.

We spend less time on traditional inherited congregations because we assume our readers are likely more familiar with them. There is, of course, no one size or shape of traditional inherited church; genuine differences pertain, even within a basic shared paradigm. We reflect on how space can be made within traditional structures for experimentation with alternative forms of Christian life, and how they can inform each other. One of the key principles of a mixed ecology is that all the elements within it work and belong together. This synergism is vital. As you read, we invite you to keep in mind those neighbors whom God loves who are disconnected from inherited forms of church and unlikely ever to encounter or attend them. It is out of our heart for them that we offer this book.

CHAPTER 1

A Time of Disconnection

Nine years into my tenure as lead pastor ("rector") at St. Matthew's Church, I (Blair) took a sabbatical. What a gift! I was freed from the daily demands of church life to embrace a different rhythm. I went through the Ignatian Exercises with a spiritual director, tried to pray for an hour each day, traveled, and began to play tennis again. I played tennis in high school, but when I returned it was a completely different game. Wood racquets were gone, as were the strokes Billy Jean King had used to defeat Bobby Riggs. It took a while to get up to speed, and for this former singles player, to learn how to volley at the net.

It was wonderful to play tennis again. It's good exercise, playful, and a way to be fully present in the moment. But what caught me by surprise was the way in which this sport provided a certain level of community in my neighborhood. The women I met and played with in drills and eventually on teams were almost exclusively ex-Catholics (when they found out I was a pastor, they started apologizing after swearing on the court!). They were raised in the Roman Catholic church, but at some point disagreed with its teachings or decided it was no longer a priority or relevant. A few started going to a local megachurch, hoping to find a service their teenagers would like and where the sermons connected with their weekday lives and realities.

Over time I witnessed my tennis team fulfilling key dimensions of a church community, minus God. We gathered weekly, cheered each other on, engaged in common practices, shared stories about our lives and families, and supported each other when there was a death, divorce, or health setback. What was missing, however, was both a spiritual component and long-term commitment. I could tell that many players hungered for this, whether they named it as God or not. Interestingly, when we made it to a national tournament, the team requested from me a prayer and blessing before our first match. Our mutual love of tennis brought us together across lines of political, class, and cultural differences.

Yet the tennis community only went so far. It was fluid. If your tennis rating went down, you got injured, or weren't around consistently, you disappeared. We were primarily there to have fun and enjoy our love for the game. It provided connection on a certain level, but without a bigger arc of meaning, service, or accountability. I watched the women care for one another, but many were at a loss when they faced a death, struggles with family members, or economic disruptions. Quietly, many confided their questions to me. Yet this kind of community could not provide the deeper support to address life's most challenging questions and realities.

This story illustrates one of the primary social dynamics unfolding in America and other Western societies today. Community is a fluid and fragile prospect for many people. Voluntary association institutions, which provided stable containers for community for many generations, are rapidly eroding. People are far less likely to join and serve them than in previous generations. We live in an increasingly "DIY" culture—people assume they need to go their own way and do it themselves. You've heard phrases like, "You be you" or "Find your truth," expressing one of the core cultural myths of late modernity, that the autonomous individual self is the ultimate authority and arbiter of truth and life. People choose to participate in organizations to serve their personal journey of self-discovery. When they feel this is not the case, they leave. Underneath all this are some cultural shifts that warrant unpacking.

The Age of Association

Let's take a quick journey back through Western cultural history.[1] Prior to the Enlightenment (which began roughly in the mid 1600s), people generally lived in a social and cultural order assumed to be given from above. Church and state were seamlessly interwoven, with a hierarchy of God, king, bishop, clergy, and aristocracy, all the way down to peasants. One's community, family, and social group defined one's identity, without much choice. Group belonging was primary and not easily renegotiable.

The Reformation, which began in the early 1500s, cracked this order open by asserting direct access to God and scripture by ordinary believers. Structures that were presumed to be divinely ordained (such as the church and state) could be reformed, renegotiated, and adapted. This was a major development that paved the way for what followed, yet the Reformation largely unfolded within *communities* who shared a basic set of assumptions, beliefs, and way of life. The resolution of the Thirty Years War (1618-48) was for each territorial area in Europe to adopt the faith of its ruler. Dissidents and religious minorities were often expelled or persecuted within a communal order that prioritized uniformity and cohesiveness.

As the Enlightenment unfolded in subsequent centuries, the individual self came to be seen as the basic unit of human life. On the one hand, this empowered the individual in ways that brought personal freedom and agency. On the other hand, it also challenged traditional structures of belonging, such as family and church, as well as traditional sources of truth and authority. For much of European history, this turn toward the individual self was constrained by the solidity of local customs, communities, and institutions, even as certain renegades and free thinkers (such as Romantic artists and bohemians) used it to chart alternative ways of belief and life.

In America, the Revolution encouraged the Enlightenment ideals of individual self-determination and led to the emergence of a new paradigm for organizing human life and community: *the voluntary association*. Rather than church and state being divinely-ordained (even if reformed) structures, they were re-envisioned as democratic associations created by individuals who entered into social contracts to accomplish the purposes of governance, social well-being, or spiritual care.[2] Individuals could join, participate, remake, and switch in and out of these associations depending on their beliefs, needs, and desires. When French diplomat, political scientist, and social theorist Alexis de Toqueville visited America in the early 19th century, he was amazed by how many Americans participated in voluntary associations.

This voluntary association paradigm unleashed a lot of creativity and innovation in church life (as well as political, social, and economic life). People were free to start new congregations and form regional judicatories, denominations, and mission societies according to their own beliefs and commitments. There was space for religious pluralism on a scale that Europe could not yet countenance. The business model for church shifted from state support to voluntary investment by individuals, whether in the form of pew rents, tithes, or offerings. People could switch congregations or denominations if they wanted. Authority came to rest in the individual, with some important exceptions. First, these voluntary associations largely remained patriarchal and exclusionary to racial minorities. Women and communities of color were forced to create their own parallel associational structures (such as women's auxiliaries or Black denominations) because they were shut out from power and participation in dominant-culture organizations. Second, for much of the 19th century through the middle of the 20th century, social conventions constrained individual personal choice and ensured high degrees of conformity.

The Age of Authenticity

Those constraints began to give way in the late 1960s when the individualistic logic of the Enlightenment took a new and more extreme trajectory. The countercultural bohemianism that had been previously restricted to certain artistic elites went mainstream, propelled by a generational rejection of the institutional and cultural conformity of the 1950s and fueled by advertising. The Baby Boomer youth rebellion of the 1960s and 70s was a rejection of the large-scale institutions created and supported by their parents and grandparents. This era brought movements that created greater equality and inclusion for groups that were marginalized and excluded in previous eras. It was also utilized by Madison Avenue to sell products by embracing the idea that individual self-expression could be found in consumer choice. Rather than conformity and fitting in, marketers sold the idea that one could stand out, express oneself, and demonstrate one's individuality through buying, wearing, driving, and displaying various products.[3]

The emergence of this new era of individual self-expression has been described by the philosopher Charles Taylor as the Age of Authenticity.[4] The premise is that a true life is found not by inhabiting a fixed place within a community and its traditions, but by discovering and expressing one's authentic self, often through rejecting structures of community and traditions. Anything that interferes with the individual's freedom to choose and perform their sense of self (as the individual defines it) is repressive and intolerable. Rather than shared communal norms and traditions passed down through generations, the emphasis shifted to self-authorship and deep skepticism toward any inherited structure, narrative, or form of external authority.

Like other forms of identity, religious identity in this emerging culture is understood to be a personal construction, and thus fluid and changeable. People understand themselves to be the author of their own stories rather than part of a story larger than themselves. Whereas religious identity used to come from the community, it is now individually chosen. Jeffrey Mahan observes, "When identity is personal, congregations do not seem essential."[5] This is accentuated by digital culture, in which everything is easily edited, transformed, and put to new purposes. People come to see the self as a digital project that is constantly being revised and reworked. Faith traditions are viewed as collections of resources individuals can adapt to serve their personal spiritual projects: "Digital culture encourages us to imagine tradition as a sort of data bank to be accessed, edited, and reused."[6]

The premise that one should have a "life of one's own" rather than conform to what everyone else does would be a bizarre concept to most people throughout history and in most cultures in the world today. It is vital that we recognize this as a culturally-specific, not universal, narrative. One of the dangers of modern Western culture is that its own cultural presuppositions are often assumed by proponents to be universal—the rest of the world will eventually be "enlightened" and catch up to the West by embracing modern Western conceptions of truth, the self, identity, and so on. This has led to all kinds of cultural and political hegemony, both historically and today.

The Age of Authenticity has brought some genuine freedoms and liberation from oppressive structures, along with a (long overdue) recognition of diversity and commitment to inclusion. Yet in a time in which postmodern philosophy purports to reject all overarching narratives ("metanarratives"), the culture of authenticity is itself just that kind of all-encompassing story. It sees life as an individual journey of self-exploration and choice, with the individual self as the ultimate authority and arbiter of truth. Anyone who would insist upon the legitimacy of shared, traditional communal truths or sources of authority beyond the self is deemed suspect, intolerant, or even oppressive. The idea that all individuals can actually freely and creatively choose their own identities, paths, and purpose is, of course, oversold. Instead, people adhere to influencers (on social media, celebrities, in politics, or elsewhere), express themselves through buying and displaying goods sold to millions of other people, and generally conform to patterns of someone else's devising.

The Age of Authenticity also places burdens on people at younger and younger ages to decide fundamental aspects of their identity (gender, sexual orientation, religion, etc.) The self is the central project of one's life—something one must continually discover, perform, express, and seek recognition for. This can lead to the anxiety of having to manage this project continually and reflexively, always looking for others to validate what is supposed to be one's own inner quest. It is a restless and precarious way to live. For all its liberating dimensions, the Age of Authenticity also brings heavy burdens to bear.

An Era of Disconnections

One of the primary signs of this shift from the Age of Association to the Age of Authenticity is a generational dis-embedding from institutional affiliation and participation without re-embedding.[7] For Baby Boomers and older generations, joining and serving voluntary associations is a natural and normal part of life. Boomers have a love/hate relationship with institutions, but engaging them is the default. For younger generations, these institutions are increasingly suspect, irrelevant, or incomprehensible. The idea that you would formally join, commit to serve, and submit to the authority of a voluntary association over time is at odds with the premises of the Age of Authenticity. Institutions may have some instrumental value, but relationships to them are fluid, changeable, and loose. Asking a millennial or Gen Z person to formally join and pledge to your congregation is a countercultural act.

For older generations alive today, joining, serving, and supporting voluntary association congregations can be deeply meaningful. Ted Smith observes that for these generations, working on the institutional church (through serving on a committee, fixing the property, volunteering to usher, etc.) was holy work. For generations steeped in the Age of Authenticity, working on the *self* is holy work.[8] Sacrificially serving institutions simply doesn't make sense, unless it feeds the self's journey of authentic discovery and expression.

Smith helpfully points out that one of the primary root causes for institutional decline in the church today is this shift from the Age of Association to the Age of Authenticity.[9] The vast majority of American inherited church structures were birthed in and designed for the Age of Association. They are reliant upon a culture that supports not only Christian identification, life, and practice, but also affiliation, participation, and service in voluntary associations. Not only is America more religiously and spiritually pluralistic and secular than in previous eras, it is also increasingly a society that is disconnecting from voluntary associations. This is affecting service organizations like Rotary, veterans' organizations, scouting, labor unions, and so many other voluntary associations—not just the church. It is a broader cultural phenomenon, not something the church has the power to reverse.

The present chaos and disintegration of American political life also reflects this shift, since our democratic structures were birthed in the Age of Association. The relocation of authority and truth to the individual self has fostered a "post-truth" environment, where people reject or are deeply skeptical of empirical and scientific claims and readily embrace conspiracy theories. Political institutions like Congress have become platforms for celebrity performance rather than policy deliberation, negotiation, and development.[10] The fabric of institutional belonging, connection, and community that Americans inherited from the Age of Association is unraveling, and it isn't clear what will replace it. While voluntary associations were indeed exclusive and problematic at times, they also provided containers for belonging, community, and service to the common good. They enabled people from different political and socio-cultural backgrounds to get to know each other, work together for shared purposes, and experience one another's humanity. What we are left with now is social media, which fosters thin connections, exacerbates tribalism, encourages bad behavior as people vie for attention and influence, and consumes as much attention for profit as possible; bureaucratic organizations (government and large corporations) that function with seemingly arbitrary power over individual and communal life; and a neo-liberal gig economy in which people are increasingly on their own to secure a livelihood. The rise of artificial intelligence will also likely bring significant economic and cultural disruption. These trends seem to be accelerating, with unpredictable consequences. Amidst all this, many yearn deeply for meaning and belonging.

Where does this leave the church? To begin with, we must acknowledge the loss involved in these cultural shifts and the resultant erosion of church structures that have been meaningful over generations. For many people in today's church (particularly older generations), watching their beloved congregation dwindle and their children and grandchildren abandon organized church participation is deeply painful. We must lament together this genuine loss. This moment invites us into the biblical narratives and practices of lament (such as in the Psalms), where we can place our grief and anger before God and recall God's faithfulness even amidst suffering.

The broader disintegration of social structures for belonging and connection in American life also means this is an opportune moment for the church to be the church. If being the church means spending all our energy trying to sustain an Age of Association institutional structure that is increasingly at odds with its cultural context, then we'll be disappointed and lose out on a huge opportunity. Is there a better time to be the church than a moment of social and cultural polarization, division, resentment, and despair? We've been here before! Just think about how Christians such as Augustine of Hippo spoke vividly of God's promises as the Roman Empire was crumbling, Francis of Assisi offered those hungering for God a simpler way of life in a time of warfare and upheaval, and Martin Luther King Jr. summoned a biblical vision of justice and reconciliation within a racist and divided America. The church is made for times like this, when the healing, freeing, reconciling gospel of Jesus can offer a life-giving alternative amidst the culture's divisive, harmful, and exhausted stories. As Christians, we meet Jesus at the foot of the cross, in the very midst of suffering, injustice, and loss, knowing that resurrection is on the horizon. We think this is a wonderful time for the church to be the church. But doing so will mean embracing some key shifts in how we imagine and go about things.

Four Key Pivots for Today's Church

Pivot in Posture: From Fixing to Listening, Discerning, and Experimenting

As Age of Association structures come under stress and unravel, the great temptation facing churches and their leaders is to assume we can fix this problem. There have been decades of attempts to reverse trends of institutional decline by applying a series of techniques, typically drawn from secular management tools and theory (usually a decade after they are introduced in the business world). This has taken the form of marketing, organizational development, family systems theory, and human-centered design thinking, for instance. We believe sociological theories, tools, and practices from the fields of organizational development, psychology, innovation, and leadership studies can be helpful to the life of the church if used carefully. Yet none of them will reverse the cultural shift from the Age of Association to the Age of Authenticity. They may improve the functioning of the church on some level, provide some insight and wisdom around organizational dynamics, and offer paths for learning and discovery. But they will not solve the deeper underlying challenge.

Moreover, this approach to fixing has a more problematic foundation: the modern Western cultural assumption that we can do it on our own. Listen to the conversation in your church's life and leadership. How often is God the acting subject of a verb? As we've listened to many churches and their leaders over the years (especially within the dominant white culture), we've found a deep tendency to stress human agency over God's agency. Modernity is built upon the wager that a good life can be lived without God.[11] The response of most churches to the cultural shifts we're describing has been to try to manage their way out of them on their own, using human expertise.

This is understandable. We've shouldered the responsibility ourselves of leading inherited church institutions designed for a different era. People expect their leaders to provide the solutions that will return their churches to a state of health, vitality, and sustainability. This is natural human behavior. Yet energy spent primarily in a fixing posture is ultimately lost energy when the reasons for the decline are out of our control and not subject to our fixing. A posture of fixing becomes a distraction from the real work we must attend to.

That work begins with *listening*—learning to listen more deeply to God through prayer and scripture, listening to the experience of the people entrusted to our care within congregations, and listening to people outside the church. A listening posture requires openness, humility (we don't know the answers yet), and intentional practices. It requires surrendering our identity as experts in charge, and becoming learners. Disciples are, after all, learners or apprentices. We must shift our posture.

We have found some specific listening practices particularly helpful for congregations to embrace. The first is Dwelling in the Word, a simple version of the ancient practice of *lectio divina* ("divine reading") that involves hearing a short Bible passage read aloud (once or twice by different voices), inviting people to pair up and share what caught their attention or what they wondered about in the text, then reporting back to the group one thing their partner shared.[12] Over time, this practice deepens participants' imaginative engagement with scripture and their capacity to listen to another person well enough to give public voice to their thoughts. In a culture of disconnection and distraction, this is fruitfully subversive.

Another key listening practice is to share spiritual stories. One of our favorite ways to do this is to invite people to reflect on a time they felt spiritually alive, energized, or engaged. They then pair up with another person and spend 5-10 minutes each sharing their story and listening carefully to their partner without trying to fix or judge. Congregations who embrace this practice typically report that members have never before been asked to reflect upon or share a story of a time they felt spiritually alive or experienced God's presence. They inevitably find it energizing. It builds their capacity to listen to their neighbors' spiritual stories outside the church.[13]

Listening can take many forms, including neighborhood prayer walks where participants pay spiritual attention to their surroundings or simple discussions with neighbors in community spaces. Through all of this listening, we can begin to *discern* more clearly God's leading. Discernment is the Christian art of "testing the spirits" to identify God's direction (1 John 4:1). Discernment is essential because there are many voices, stories, and influences seeking to form us, not all of them faithful and holy. Practicing discernment means prayerfully and carefully naming where we see God at work in our midst and in the neighborhood, interpreting our experience in light of scripture, and identifying God's call to us, both personally and communally.

The posture of listening and discerning rather than fixing has another dimension, *experimenting*. Experimenting is a way to discover solutions for challenges we don't know the answers to ahead of time. When challenges have no easy answers (such as those facing the church today), experiments are vital. They involve behaving our way into new ways of thinking and believing, rather than just trying to come up with solutions in the abstract. To experiment is to risk ourselves as learners, but within parameters of relative safety. We understand that fostering a culture of experimentation can feel especially vulnerable right now when local churches face so many challenges, but learning more about the future God is bringing forth through experimentation is critical.

The kinds of experiments the church needs today should be grounded in listening and discernment. When we experiment, we begin with a question we're seeking the answer to. We identify some actions (not too many!) we can take to gather input and feedback—to learn. Then we reflect on what took place and name what we discovered. For congregations, these experiments should normally be small, low-cost, able to fail, and on the edges of the church's life.[14] Many of the stories of innovative forms of Christian community and witness we describe in this book should be understood as fundamentally experimental. They function on the edges of the life of inherited church structures, where ordinary life happens. They are addressing the core challenge of learning how to form Christian identity, practice, and community in today's cultural environment.

Pivot in Focus: From Membership to Discipleship

The challenge of forming Christian community today is the core challenge facing the church. In the era of Western Christendom (when Christianity was socially, culturally, and politically privileged), the surrounding culture was assumed to be Christian and to support Christian identity and practice. This made the formation of disciples (apprentices, learners) less of a central focus. Many churches assumed that participation in worship once a week, while important, would form people in Christ more than it actually does. Moreover, the voluntary association model of church life was easily redirected toward other purposes than forming disciples of Jesus. Alongside the pivot in posture from fixing to listening, discerning, and experimenting is a pivot in *focus*, from gaining and engaging voluntary association members to cultivating apprentices of Jesus's way of life and love.

For many Age of Association churches, the focus has been on attracting and retaining members, not unlike other voluntary associations in the broader society. Getting people to attend worship or programs, formally join, contribute financially, and serve as volunteers constitutes success. Leaders are expected to dedicate their time and energy to these priorities, which are typically measured by denominations and regional church bodies. The problem is that one can do all these things and not become a disciple of Jesus or grow deeper spiritually (defined as increasing in love of God and neighbor).

Research conducted in both evangelical and mainline churches bears this out. The Reveal study conducted initially 20 years ago by Willow Creek Community Church in suburban Chicago and implemented later in hundreds of other churches found no correlation between increased participation in church programs and activities and spiritual growth.[15] RenewalWorks, an Episcopal organization, found that only 5 percent of over 29,000 Episcopalians in over 350 congregations consider themselves to be centered on a life with Jesus. Only 24 percent are beginning to embrace a personal relationship with God (over mere church membership) and the remaining 71 percent consider themselves to be at an early stage of spiritual maturity. Most of these respondents have been Episcopalians for a long time and participate actively in their churches. A majority (59 percent) want their local church to help them go deeper spiritually, but most do not feel their congregations are doing so.[16] It is striking that the other 41 percent *don't* want their local church to help them grow spiritually! They are there for other purposes.

Functionally, many congregations are focused primarily on social and cultural aims rather than growing followers of Jesus. Church may be where people see their friends and experience a sense of community at coffee hour or through a men's or women's group. Churches may be institutions that preserve a specific cultural heritage (lutefisk or Swedish meatball suppers in

Lutheran churches, kirkin' o' the Tartan in Presbyterian churches, etc.). They may pass down a particular aesthetic tradition in terms of music, architecture, or liturgy. Or perhaps they serve as a vehicle for community service. If you ask people what primary work the church does in their lives, many will likely name these things. While they are not bad in themselves, they are not the same as learning how to follow Jesus as a disciple in today's world.

Following Jesus is a holistic way of life. It unfolds in relationships—with God through the power of the Spirit, with mentors and guides, with other disciples in community, and with neighbors in the world. It is both Jesus's first invitation to his followers at the beginning of his ministry ("Come, follow me," Mark 1:17) and his final command to them at the end ("Go therefore and make disciples of all nations, baptizing them in the name of the Father and of the Son and of the Holy Spirit, and teaching them to obey everything that I have commanded you," Matthew 28:19-20). Following Jesus is the central thing Christians are supposed to do. But it is not what most churches are organized around.

John Mark Comer notes how far Jesus's model of apprenticeship is from the modern Western educational system:

> To follow Jesus meant to walk alongside him in a posture of listening, learning, observation, obedience, and imitation. For Jesus's first apprentices the goal wasn't to pass a test, get a degree, or receive a certificate to frame on your office wall; it was to master the art of living in God's good world by learning from Jesus how to make

> steady progress into the kingdom of God. It was less like learning chemistry and more like learning jujitsu.[17]

Comer goes on to point out that the word "Christian" is used only three times in the New Testament, while the word "disciple" (or "apprentice") is used 269 times. Somehow, we have missed the point of church at a colossal level; the church's life and witness have been deeply compromised as a result.

Many congregations offer no clear vision of what following Jesus entails in daily life. They assume that participation in worship (often relatively passively) or a few classes automatically translates into deeper growth into Christlikeness. What might it mean to *center* discipleship as the primary focus of the church? Eun Strawser begins with relationships of mentoring in a community that help people live a Jesus-shaped life in relation to neighbors. This can lay a very different foundation for a new church than focusing initially on worship.[18] The discipleship challenge is foundational to addressing the other challenges facing churches in Western contexts today.

Pivot in Structure: From One Model Fits All to a Mixed Ecology

In the 20th century, the Age of Association model of church became standardized in many ways. Along the lines of many businesses and other organizations in American life, churches adopted a franchise model. Denominations offered standardized liturgical resources, hymnals, Sunday school curricula, and even architectural plans for church buildings. In many communities, the basic model was that of a congregation with a dedicated building, a professionally-trained pastor or two and small staff, and status as a 501(c)3 nonprofit organization. Pastors were trained and credentialed as professionals according to standardized criteria, with the assumption they could function in any congregation across the denomination, like interchangeable parts in a big machine.

Following World War II, the suburban boom brought a wave of church planting in which denominations purchased lots in housing developments, set up signs indicating the date a new denominational church would open, and members of that denomination moving into the area would show up to form a church. This model had exceptions and variations. Rural and urban congregations had their own versions, with varying degrees of uniformity depending on local context and history. Churches in communities of color often utilized business models that didn't assume a full-time, paid pastor or staff. Yet the trend overall was toward a high degree of standardization across American Christianity. If you asked most people on the street, "church" was a building where certain religious rituals were offered by clergy on Sunday during a fixed couple of hours each week.

This basic paradigm carries forward the long-established parish system from European Christianity, in which local areas are divided into geographical units, each with its dedicated parish church. Within the Christendom state church model, everyone born within that geographical parish was automatically a "member" of the parish church. Records of births and deaths were maintained in the local parish register. In America, denominational parish structures overlapped in more complicated ways.

We live in a moment when the inherited voluntary association structure with its standardization is not working to form Christian community with the whole diverse variety of people who inhabit today's neighborhoods. Let us be clear: we affirm that these forms of church work meaningfully for some, but this is increasingly the case for fewer people. A single model of church (especially a standardized one) cannot reflect the cultural, religious, and social diversity present in today's America or other Western societies. The standardized denominational franchise church system is breaking down rapidly.

We need to pivot in structure from a one-model-fits-all paradigm to a mixed ecology. In the following chapters, we explore some of the alternatives that are emerging consisting of multiple forms of Christian community and witness existing simultaneously. Alongside inherited models are various forms of church plants, fresh expressions, megachurches, microchurches, and digital churches. They all have opportunities and risks, just like the traditional structures. But we cannot expect the inherited voluntary association parish church model to reach many people who have no experience of church, have rejected (or been harmed by) traditional churches, or find the typical Sunday morning worship service inaccessible. The church has to figure out how to meet neighbors where they are and speak their language.

Pivot in Leadership: From Primarily Clergy-Led, Lay-Supported, to Lay-Led, Clergy-Supported

One of the products of Christendom was the clericalization of ministry. In the New Testament, the church is a community of people learning to follow Jesus, with a variety of spiritual gifts distributed throughout its members (see especially Romans 12 and 1 Corinthians 12). The Spirit gives gifts to some to be apostles, prophets, evangelists, pastors, and teachers, in order to equip the whole body of believers for ministry as they grow into spiritual maturity in Christ (Ephesians 4:11-13). Scripture talks about the church as Jesus's body, with each part integral to the healthy functioning of the whole. There are leaders, but no separate caste of clergy in the New Testament. This was a later development when the church went from being a countercultural community to a religious institution within a (purportedly) Christian society, and adopted hierarchical leadership structures from the Roman Empire.

Within the modern Western voluntary association institutional paradigm of church, ministry also became professionalized.[19] Clergy were the "ministers" who did ministry for the congregation; the social contract for church members was to provide and maintain an institutional home for clergy to do it in. The spiritual work was primarily performed for the congregation by the clergy. In most cases, regular members ("laity") were expected to support the church institutionally with their "time, talent, and treasure" rather than to be fluent at praying, interpreting the Bible, or evangelism themselves. Many church members have been happy to let clergy do the spiritual work on their behalf. Professional clergy training has tended to focus on how to *do* ministry within an institutional context (how to preach, put together a service, and provide pastoral care), not how to equip and cultivate gift-based ministry and mission among all God's people.

This understanding of ordained ministry is functionally breaking down as the voluntary association model of church and professional model of ministry come under stress. About 43 percent of U.S. mainline congregations have no full-time paid clergy, according to the 2018-19 National Congregations Study.[20] As of 2016, a quarter of Evangelical Lutheran Church in America (ELCA) congregations could no longer afford a full-time pastor with benefits.[21] Almost half of Episcopal churches are led by part-time or non-paid clergy or lay leaders.[22] These trends are accelerating, leading one Presbyterian (USA) pastor to describe the future of her denomination as "pastor-less, and that's OK."[23]

What is already widespread in many places in the church is a lay-led, clergy-supported model of ministry. This may take the form of a pastor or priest overseeing multiple lay-led congregations in a region. Or it may be a part-time or non-stipendiary clergy person equipping and mentoring teams of lay leaders exercising gift-based ministry within a single local church. Many of the innovative forms of church we describe later are predominantly lay-led. Lay leadership is the norm in many places in the global majority church where Christianity is thriving and growing exponentially.

These four pivots belong together. For churches birthed in and designed for a different cultural era than we find ourselves in today, they will represent a stretch, a reorientation, and a significant renegotiation of established norms and expectations. This ultimately involves a shift in culture, which is never easy. Yet, as we unpack in the next chapter, the church has been through such transformations before.

CHAPTER 2

Rediscovering Roots

During the period of slavery in the American South, enslaved African Christians stole away at night into "hush harbors" in order to experience Christian worship and community in cultural forms and with messages meaningful to them. The church of their slave masters often preached a distorted gospel of white supremacy and the submission of subordinates (slaves and women). In response, enslaved Christians created their own expression of church away from the slave masters' eyes and reach. It took place in secret, secluded places (often out in the woods), with muffled voices, at hours when masters and overseers were asleep. It happened at great risk of severe punishment or death.

The hush harbor church looked and sounded different from the master's church. Biblical passages about God's liberation of God's people from slavery and oppression (such as the Exodus narratives) came to the forefront. God's biblical promises of freedom, release, and eternal restoration to community with God and loved ones in heaven were lifted up. God's justice for marginalized and suffering people was proclaimed. Preaching, song, and prayer could take on ecstatic and Spirit-filled expressions. Dancing and drums native to participants' African cultural heritage were integral to worship in ways that were forbidden in the white church. Hearing a message of liberation, knowing they were seen by God, and being reminded that God ultimately has the last word gave enslaved people the hope, encouragement, and dignity they needed to persist. Hush harbors were an "invisible institution" that coexisted alongside and under the radar of the dominant culture church, which had lost its faithfulness to the gospel by adopting the narratives, assumptions, and practices of slaveholding culture.[1]

Throughout church history, Christians have wrestled with how to faithfully embody the gospel in different cultural situations and historical moments. Many times, they have gotten it wrong. Often in those situations, minority groups of believers take the risk of claiming and living out a faithful gospel witness in the face of resistance from dominant social and cultural institutions. This is, of course, where the church began in relation to the Roman Empire and to mainstream Judaism. When the church has worldly power, it tends to be more liable to distort its understanding and embodiment of and witness to the gospel of Christ. This chapter explores the complicated relationship of gospel and culture, reflects critically on the predominant culture of the late modern West, and identifies examples from Christian history demonstrating that the mixed ecology is nothing new.

Contextualization: The Word Made Flesh in Local Culture

The church is the body of Christ in the world, animated by the Holy Spirit. This simple premise is a radical concept and a complex reality to inhabit. The world is God's good creation, which includes the variety of human cultures. These cultures all have the capacity to bear God's presence and promises. The world is also distorted by sin, or estrangement from and disobedience to God, and human cultures reflect this. The church is both holy and human; it is part of creation, and reflects this tension between creaturely goodness and the liability to be distorted by sin.

The long pattern of God's faithful love of God's people in scripture is a story of *particularity*—God working through specific people in concrete historical circumstances to accomplish God's purposes. One of the remarkable messages of the Bible is that God creates and redeems the world through ordinary people and ordinary life. Paul talks about how scandalous this concept was to the Greek philosophical culture of his day, which tended to abstract the true, good, and beautiful away from the messiness of regular life into a distant realm of ideas and pure being.

The incarnation of Jesus is God's ultimate embrace of human particularity, local culture, and ordinary life. In order to restore humanity's participation in and right relationship with the life of the Trinity, God participates fully in human life in the incarnation. "The Word became flesh and blood and moved into the neighborhood" (John 1:14).[2] The incarnation is God's definitive entry into local culture, following a long tradition throughout the Bible of God's patient engagement with particular people in particular places. As Lesslie Newbigin points out, this embrace of particular people and particular cultures is not meant to privilege those people or cultures above others, but rather to call them into responsibility and service on behalf of the whole.[3] Just as Abraham and Sarah are "blessed to be a blessing" (Genesis 12:1-3), so too are Israel and the church.

Andrew Walls observes that the incarnation is a kind of translation of divinity into humanity. Yet there is no universal or abstract human life, language, or culture—only specific ones.[4] Jesus became a first-century Palestinian Jew. He spoke the everyday language of people in his context and used metaphors, images, and terms familiar to that world. Jesus announced the arrival of God's reign or kingdom in language that both resonated with longstanding expectations of his fellow Jews for a savior or messiah, and also redefined and subverted those expectations. He embodied Good News (gospel) in ways that challenged both the Jewish and Greco-Roman cultural narratives and assumptions of his time. Rather than a military or political hero or philosopher detached from the messiness of life, Jesus came as a suffering servant. As Newbigin reminds us, "There can never be a culture-free gospel. Yet the gospel, which is from the beginning to the end embodied in culturally conditioned forms, calls into question all cultures, including the one in which it was originally embodied."[5]

What does all this mean for the church today? First, it is important to recognize that the Christian church has taken and must take countless different cultural forms through different times and places if it is to be the body of Christ incarnationally and speak in the vernacular. The church's universality ("catholicity," or wholeness) must always be expressed through particularity. Otherwise, it will not faithfully embody Christ in its local environment. It is remarkable that very few Christians today speak the language that Jesus spoke—Aramaic. Some religions insist that the language and culture of their founder are normative for all subsequent followers. This has never been the case for Christianity. Already within the New Testament itself we have translation taking place into Greek. This is a prelude to ongoing translation of the gospel and the body of Christ into local cultures and languages everywhere in the world and throughout history.[6] This process is called *contextualization*—the faithful presence and embodiment of the body of Christ in varying cultural contexts.

Contextualization isn't easy, however. Because the church is full of humans who are not immune from sin, and all local cultures have deep narratives, assumptions, and practices that stand in tension with the gospel, the church sometimes gets this wrong. Imagine a road with two ditches, one on either side. The road, or "way," is incarnation, or faithful contextualization (Jesus describes himself as the "the way" in John 14:6 and Acts refers to the early Christian movement as "the way"). On that road, the Word becomes flesh in local languages and cultures in ways that are accessible to people, yet also challenges whatever in local cultures contradicts Jesus's holistic way of life and love.

On one side of the road is the ditch of *under-contextualization*, where the church doesn't inhabit local cultures and languages deeply enough to speak clearly to people. In order to follow Jesus or engage the church, people have to migrate out of their native culture. The history of Western colonial mission is full of problematic examples of this. Think of the pipe organs imposed on African believers who were told to leave their drums at the door by European missionaries.

On the other side of the road is the ditch of *over-contextualization*, where the church embraces local culture and language so deeply that it loses the distinctiveness of the gospel (accommodation or syncretism are other terms for this). In this case, the culture's narratives and practices are uncritically adopted and the gospel becomes subservient to them. Think of the state Lutheran church in Germany during the Nazi era or the Dutch Reformed Church supporting apartheid in South Africa.

Sometimes, the same church or church tradition can fall into both ditches simultaneously. For instance, in the American context many mainline churches are under-contextualized in their worship (speaking the language of medieval cathedrals, Shakespearean English, and 19th century hymns) while being over-contextualized in their theology (embracing modern Western culture's narratives of expressive individualism and relativism). Some conservative evangelical churches reflect a reverse version of this. They are over-contextualized in their worship (church looks like a shopping mall or rock concert, songs focus on an individual's romance with Jesus), while being under-contextualized in their theology (people are expected to embrace modern fundamentalist views of the literal scientific validity of the creation accounts in scripture, for instance). It is easy to get this wrong!

Excavating Deeper Cultural Narratives

As the era of Christendom unravels, churches in Western societies must reflect more deeply on the cultures in which they find themselves. During the Christendom era, it was easy to assume the surrounding culture was basically Christian and that the primary work of evangelism and mission took place somewhere else (in global majority contexts, for instance), or focused merely on addressing physical needs through social ministries. There was much less recognition of the need to share the gospel with neighbors.

Lesslie Newbigin (1909-98) was an English Reformed pastor who spent much of his life as a missionary in India, living among the local people, learning how to articulate the gospel of Jesus in language and forms that made sense to the people he worked with. For instance, he recognized that if you say, "Jesus is Lord" to a Hindu, the response will typically be something like, "Sure, there are millions of lords in the Hindu pantheon; let's add Jesus to that group." The preexisting cultural framework subsumed the distinctiveness of what Christians mean when we say that Jesus is Lord of all. Or, if you talk about the incarnation, Hindus will understand this in terms of the cycles of reincarnation.[7] Newbigin eventually became bishop of the Church of South India and a beloved figure in that context. When he retired to England, he realized that the West had become a mission field. Western culture was no longer primarily shaped by the gospel of Jesus. Newbigin asked a provocative question: "Can the West be converted?"[8]

Given the pervasive globalized influence of Western culture, Newbigin asserted that Western culture is the most dangerous foe the church has faced in its long history.[9] There is a myth in the West that we live in a neutral culture with no creed. Yet, as Michael Goheen and Timothy Sheridan note, "The metanarrative of Western humanism is not neutral: it offers a comprehensive vision of life that demands ultimate allegiance."[10] What are the elements of this deeper cultural vision that shape the life of the church in Western contexts today?

First is the assumption that humans are basically good and can use their own abilities to bring about progress and perfection for the world. Goheen and Sheridan write, "Humanity builds this paradise and humans save themselves by science, technology, economics, and politics. Universal reason is emancipated from dogma and disciplined by the scientific method to conquer all the evils that enslave men and women. . .. All this will achieve a new world."[11] This kind of cultural faith emerged in the European Enlightenment and became the default position in Western culture.

In this worldview, the public sphere of scientific "facts" is separated from the private sphere of individual "values." The former is supposed to be objective and empirically verifiable, the latter subjective and relative. Autonomous individuals are supposed to work out their own salvation through economic self-realization (unlimited material growth) and self-expression (through consumerism and identity construction). In this cultural creed, Christian faith is relegated to private, individual preference (as long as it doesn't interfere with the "neutral," "objective" public sphere).

During the course of the 20th century, the founding Enlightenment optimism about objective truth and human perfectibility was called into question by the first and second World Wars, in which people harnessed all that brilliant science and technology to kill each other at a previously unimaginable scale. What emerged afterward was a deeper turn toward relativism and a sense of the instability of all sources of truth, which were seen to be simply assertions of power. This very conception has itself become a defining cultural narrative of late modernity or postmodernity. Rather than look outside of ourselves for any source of truth that would anchor human life and society, there is a radical inward turn. We are seeing this play out today in the predominance of expressive individualism, which sees life as a journey of individual self-discovery and performance without accountability to external sources. It is playing into the disconnection from shared communal norms and structures of belonging and the "DIY" culture described in the last chapter. In this cultural story, the individual human self is the ultimate authority.

William Cavanagh argues that in the modern West the sacred has not actually been drained from the world but moved from the church to the state and marketplace: "Worship has not receded in a supposedly 'secular' world, but has rather migrated from the explicit worship of God to the implicit worship of the things of human creation."[12] He argues that the modern Western myth that humans are in charge is deeply false, because human life is subject to all kinds of cultural, social, and economic forces out of our control: "Humans are not in charge, but are being ruled by a god of their own making."[13] This takes the form of consumerism and nationalism most acutely in his eyes. Cavanaugh describes the crowds lining up at midnight on Black Friday to rush into a Best Buy electronics store as an example of a kind of secular consumerist liturgy. Transcendence has been turned toward imminent things, which become charged with a kind of magical quality. While the premise of late modernity is that individuals are free to choose from endless options for their lives, consumerism functions as an overarching, unquestionable assumption.[14] Within this framework, religious identity and participation also become matters of individual consumer choice rather than ultimate sources of meaning and public truth.

Idolatry is the worship of anything other than the creator, who alone is ultimate. It is a helpful category through which to understand the cultural forces we've just named and how they shape us. Western culture is neither universal nor neutral. It is fraught with faith claims and formative influences that catechize people into its image. Christianity emerged in contrast to the idolatries of first-century pagan society, which elevated empire, hedonism, militarism, wealth, and power. Contemporary Western culture is full of idolatries. To the extent to which the church uncritically embraces and reflects these forces, its identity and mission are compromised. If the Bible and the Christian story are relegated to private sources for life optimization within the larger cultural framework of consumerism and self-actualization, their power will be lost. If the church simply echoes and amplifies what the wider culture is offering (on the right and on the left), no wonder it is diminishing in engagement, participation, and relevance.

Can the West Be Converted?

What does a missionary encounter with Western culture look like? It begins with recovering the gospel as *public* and *narrative* truth. Newbigin says, "If the biblical story is not the one that controls our thinking, then inevitably we shall be swept into the story the world tells about itself. We shall become increasingly indistinguishable from the pagan world of which we are a part."[15] When we talk about the Bible as the source of truth, this means a narrative series of historical events, not just a compendium of propositions or life principles. Jesus is truth as a *person* through the historical events of his life, death, and resurrection. Christianity is not a set of abstract ideas, but a way of life in relationship with a living God and a community that is both local and extends through space and time.[16]

To place the human self at the center of truth, authority, and goodness is idolatrous. One of the reasons why there is such widespread loneliness, anxiety, and despair in Western societies right now is because the individual self is a very shaky foundation upon which to build meaning, community, and human flourishing. If there is no transcendent reality to deliver us from ourselves, we are in trouble indeed.

Ultimately, this applies to the church as well. Late modernity has fostered the assumption that the church can save itself from whatever challenges it faces. Christendom made the church primarily concerned about its own institutional life rather than offering a faithful witness to its neighbors. All the energy being spent trying to fix established church structures from the Christendom and voluntary association eras will not actually yield much fruit. Instead, the church must figure out what it means to be the body of Christ living Jesus's way in a culture that is deeply at odds with the Christian story. Cavanaugh writes, "The best remedy for idolatry is an uncontrollable encounter with the incarnate God in the chaos and vulnerability of those who are marginalized by the idolatrous systems that eat people alive."[17]

This is where the promise of intercultural relationships among Christians is vital to claim.[18] For instance, many global majority world cultures reject Western modernity's dualistic bifurcation of the spiritual and material. Reality is experienced in a more holistic, integrated way, similar to what we read in the Bible. The stories of Jesus's healings in the Gospels touch on restoring not only bodily or mental health but also spiritual wholeness and reconnection to community. This is not at all strange to some African cultures, for instance, that view all reality as spiritual. In many African churches, there tends to be a vibrant expectation that these biblical stories speak directly to human experience and struggle in the here and now, and that the Holy Spirit can bring deliverance from evil.[19]

Over the past half century, many churches in the American context have tended to respond to the disintegration of both Christendom and the voluntary association model of church on the terms of the surrounding culture. Many white mainline churches began losing cultural centrality in the 1960s and embraced expressive individualism by adopting a therapeutic approach to theology, spirituality, and ministry. Clergy who could no longer play the role of authoritative religious figures at the center of their communities redefined themselves as advisors helping individuals discover and realize their true selves. At the same time, many Black churches were engaged in a holistic struggle in the Civil Rights movement, connecting God's deliverance in the biblical narrative to God's action in the present to bring about justice in the community and nation. Some predominantly white churches joined them, while others resisted.

Political activism became in subsequent decades for some churches on the theological left a primary way to discover energy, purpose, and identity in an increasingly secular culture. While social engagement has always been part of faithful Christian witness, many of these churches struggled to clearly articulate the difference Jesus makes and how the church is distinct from other nonprofit organizations in these struggles. These churches sought to legitimize themselves to (certain segments of) society by participating in progressive movements for social change. Sometimes, there were explicit biblical and theological rationales for this engagement, but other times churches have simply adopted and reflected secular cultural ideologies. This hasn't addressed the underlying identity crisis for such churches, since you don't need a pastor for therapy or a congregation for activism.

Conservative evangelical churches had their own versions of seeking legitimacy on Western culture's grounds. Many embraced business techniques of marketing, entrepreneurship, and sales to drive church growth. Expanding religious "market share" through attracting more members became a focus of energy, attention, and status. Pastors adopted celebrity culture and promoted themselves, affirming the cult of personality ethos of late modern media culture. Churches tailored their experience toward individual consumption, with worship music that was all about the individual believer's intimacy with Jesus and a lot less about the world God so loves. Salvation was about getting my individual self into heaven instead of the reconciliation of all people and all creation to God and each other. With the recent wave of pastor scandals and a rise in social consciousness among younger evangelicals, these approaches are becoming exhausted.

The problem with all of this—on the left and the right—is that these approaches fundamentally miss the deeper challenge of cultivating Christian identity, practice, and community in a culture that has rejected the gospel. Again, minority communities less dominated by Western Enlightenment culture have often stayed faithfully on the "way" rather than falling into these ditches. They know what it is to inhabit a foreign and resistant culture, and what kinds of stories and practices retain, renew, and sustain a distinct identity. Perhaps most importantly, they are more likely to rely upon God's power, presence, and leading to deliver them and provide a hopeful future that is not assumed to be primarily of human making.

Contextualization of Church Life and Structure

Church community life and structure are themselves always culturally embodied and vary over time. When the church is faithfully incarnate, it shares deeply in the life of the local community and context while centering its life around stories and practices that subvert dominant cultural narratives. For instance, while table fellowship in the Greco-Roman context of the first century normally reflected social stratification, early Christians broke bread in homes across social, economic, and cultural lines. Early Christians distributed goods and money according to need at a time when many people lived with financial insecurity as the empire extracted resources from the peoples it had conquered to fund its military conquests, bureaucracy, and elites. Early Christians rescued and raised unwanted infants abandoned to die, which was a common practice at the time, demonstrating a powerful commitment to the value of human life amidst a culture of death.

These Christians started where life was already happening—in homes, workplaces, markets, synagogues, and eventually

Roman civic assembly spaces. They took on and transformed the leadership and organizational structures at hand. For instance, the leadership offices of first-century synagogues form the basis of much of what we find in the New Testament for leadership roles, with some adaptations.[20] Craig Ott and Gene Wilson write,

> Relatively few details regarding church structure are biblically prescribed; rather, the focus is primarily on purposes and values. From this, along with the decision of the Jerusalem Council (Acts 15), we deduce that congregations were given considerable freedom in the specifics of how church life should be structured. New Testament churches *had* to be very flexible and resilient, because in most cases they emerged in hostile territory and had to adapt to changing circumstances.[21]

Flexibility and adaptation characterize the centuries of early Christian history, as followers of Jesus sought to embody his way in all kinds of cultures. The church adopted successive, hierarchical orders of ministry (bishop, priest, deacon) from the Roman imperial career ladder (*cursus honorum*), along with the diocese as a unit of governance. The parish structure emerged within the paradigm of Christendom as a way of demarcating bounds of pastoral responsibility and community life.

If the local neighborhood church became the basic unit of Christian belonging and practice within Western societies as they came to embrace Christianity at a large scale, there were impulses that could not be contained within it. Christianity went from being a marginal movement with high barriers to entry (long catechetical process, strict moral standards, and countercultural practices for believers) to the default religion in society after the Roman Empire's embrace of it. This led some believers who wanted to live a deeper, more pure, and focused Christian life out into the desert and monastic communities. These monasteries (with many local variations) embodied a shared rule of life, daily worship, commitment to deep relationships over time, and practices that addressed core human temptations. To counter the impulse to take and hoard power over others, monks and nuns vowed obedience to the community, its rule, and leadership (in the form of the abbess or abbot). To counteract lust, monastics took vows of celibacy. To deal with greed, they vowed simplicity and poverty.

When monasticism itself became highly institutionalized in Medieval Europe, groups of laywomen known as *Beguines* began to form communities outside and alongside the established parish and monastic structures. These women sought to live a holy life together in community, supported by their own labor. The Beguines engaged scripture in the vernacular, which was controversial at the time. Whereas many established convents required women to bring significant resources with them for their support, thus excluding poorer women, the Beguines welcomed all.[22] They focused their lives on discipleship, spiritual growth, and service to the poor and sick in the local neighborhood. For instance, Mary of Oignies (1177-1213), the leader of a Beguine community in Northern France, founded one of the first hospitals in Europe.[23] These communities came into conflict with the established religious authorities as they offered a compelling incarnational witness in their settings.

In the 18th century, when established Protestant state churches in Northern Europe became highly focused on correct doctrine, Pietists developed communities such as Herrnhut in Germany where Christians practiced an alternative way of life. They stressed engagement with scripture, spiritual practices, practical living out of the faith, and mutual accountability, often through small group structures. Rather than moving these impulses out of daily life in the world like many monastic movements, Pietism sought to bring a deeper holiness into everyday living in the world.

John Wesley was a Christian leader influenced by Pietism who went on to found what became the Methodist movement. Raised and ordained in the Church of England, Wesley sought to activate a heartfelt, lived Christian faith that resulted in a changed life and service to the poor. When he was prevented from preaching in Church of England pulpits, Wesley went out into fields and town squares to share the Good News of God's transforming love in Jesus with anyone interested. He also cultivated a whole system of smaller groups, each with its own level of spiritual intimacy, that could help people grow in their discipleship. In introductory small groups ("trial bands") people could become more aware of God's grace at work in their lives. They were expected to learn how to practice life in Christian community through confession, forgiveness, mutual support, and encouragement. They could then progress to larger "class" structures where they learned the basics of the Christian faith and experienced deeper conversion. Some then joined more advanced small groups ("bands") where they went deeper in their discipleship with mutual accountability and service toward others. A final small group structure ("select bands") were devoted to "sanctifying grace" as people participated in divine intimacy and grew into holiness.[24] The open-air preaching and smaller structures to support discipleship challenged established church authorities and systems and led to a powerful global movement of Christian renewal.

In the second half of the 20th century, Base Ecclesial Communities (BECs) emerged in Latin American contexts within the Roman Catholic Church, primarily among the poor. BECs empowered ordinary lay believers to engage scripture, reflect on its implications for their daily lives and situations, and grow in their discipleship. As with Hush Harbors, BECs claimed and amplified passages of scripture that highlighted God's care for the poor and oppressed and themes of God's justice and liberation. BECs met and continue to meet in homes or other local neighborhood spaces, and in contexts where priests can be rare, they have fostered lay leadership. BECs have been in tension with the Roman Catholic hierarchy at various points, particularly over their embrace of liberation theology, but have also found support and encouragement there too.[25]

Christianity in China became a significant force in the early 20th century through the influence of indigenous preachers. When the Chinese Communist Party came to power in 1949, many Chinese Christians came under its control. Others refused to register with the official Protestant or Catholic bodies and continued to meet secretly and illegally. Since they started doing so mostly in homes, the movement of Chinese Christian churches resisting state control are known as the "house church" movement (though some meet in other spaces). Today, the house church movement in China is diverse theologically and growing exponentially, providing a powerful countercultural witness as the

Chinese government increasingly exerts control and uniformity on all aspects of life. Like BECs, Chinese house churches have learned how to raise up and mobilize local leaders.[26]

In many places in Africa where Christianity is growing rapidly, evangelists and catechists lead local church communities under the oversight of a pastor who may be responsible for overseeing as many as a dozen of these smaller congregations. This works in part because every Christian is responsible for doing the work of evangelism, visitation, praying for the sick, and other ministry duties. The clergy focus on equipping, but the work of ministry is broadly shared across the community.[27]

Conclusion

Reviewing these examples from church history, we see that there is no one size or shape for Christian community, even as there are shared values, stories (especially scripture), and practices. Being the body of Christ in a changing cultural context means discerning how to practice Jesus's way faithfully in a particular time and place. We are likely to get it wrong when we aren't engaging deeply and regularly with scripture, when we are tempted by worldly power, prestige, and recognition, and when we disconnect from Christians in other cultures who can help us see our cultural captivity. We can see through history that when the church becomes too caught up in its own structure, bureaucracy, or the surrounding culture, the Spirit raises up Christian communities on the margins to embody a faithful witness.

Churches in Western contexts today have basic work to do to rediscover gospel faithfulness after the long legacy of Christendom and within the context of late modern culture. This is the work of deepening discipleship and spiritual practices through things faithful Christians have always done—gathering together to read and discuss the Bible as the normative story, praying with expectation that God acts in our lives and world, offering our lives and selves in worship to God in a posture of gratitude and to remind ourselves that we are not the center of the universe, sacrificially giving and serving one another and the poor in love, confessing our sins and receiving forgiveness from God and one another, and learning how to live justly as stewards of this Earth. Many established church structures and systems are not primarily organized around this basic work for ordinary believers in daily life. Paying attention to expressions of church within minority communities or experimental forms on the edges of the church's life can yield hopeful insight for what faithfulness looks like.

Yet looking internally only takes us so far. If we aren't engaged with our neighbors who are outside the institutional church, we will miss out on what God is doing in our contexts and likely fall prey to institutional worries and insider concerns. This is a moment when we must take seriously what it means to be a church on mission, a church sent into the world in love and witness as the body of Christ in the power of the Spirit. But that mission must not be the imperial mission of Christendom and colonialism; it must begin from a humbler, simpler, more vulnerable place. It is on the edges of the church's life—in the boundary spaces—that God is innovating a new future. It is on the margins that the church must rediscover its identity and calling.

CHAPTER 3

Church Planting

We visited IMPRINT Church in London for worship on a Sunday afternoon. IMPRINT is a church plant that started in Leicester, a city in the East Midlands of England, and now also meets in the financial district of London (known as Bank). Meeting in St. Edmund the King, a Sir Christopher Wren church full of imperial and royal imagery, the congregation is predominantly comprised of young people of color. On the wall, we noticed a list of vicars (priests) going back hundreds of years. After the early 1990s, it was blank. Before IMPRINT began to use the building, St. Edmund the King had long ceased to have a congregation. Baptisms hadn't been performed in over 40 years.

IMPRINT began with a dream its founding leader, Wole Agbaje, had several nights in a row. The dream featured offering a showcase of the gospel through drama, dance, spoken word, and music to university students in Leicester, where he lived at the time. Agbaje worked with other local Christians to put the showcase on, and it was a success. It led to hundreds of young adults becoming connected to a university student ministry. With encouragement and equipping from mentors in his local Church of England congregation, Agbaje planted IMPRINT out of this student ministry in Leicester. As it continued to grow, IMPRINT's leadership felt called to plant in London. Agbaje was told, "Bank is where church plants go to die" because few people live there, even as thousands come in and out of the neighborhood each day for work. But trusting God's call, he and a team began with showcases and what they call "Crews" (small groups), which led to IMPRINT being invited by Bishop Ric Thorpe to plant in Bank using three dormant church buildings—St. Edmund the King, St. Mary Woolnoth, and St. Clement Eastcheap.

Today, IMPRINT offers multiple worship services, Bible studies, and other programming in these spaces each week, primarily for a diverse group of young professionals, creatives, and the occasional tourist who wanders in. The worship is contemplative-charismatic and soulful. St. Mary Woolnoth is where John Newton (author of the hymn "Amazing Grace") was vicar in the late 1700s. Newton mentored William Wilberforce, an Anglican politician, in bringing an end to the slave trade in the British Empire. IMPRINT recently helped commemorate the 250th anniversary of "Amazing Grace." Agbaje started IMPRINT in his 20s and completed his theological training at St. Mellitus College in London while leading the church. The church currently has multiple interns as it raises up the next generation of leaders. Within the shells of old church buildings at what was once the heart of Christendom and empire, the Spirit of God is creating a new Christian community through IMPRINT, reflecting the global majority present in this cosmopolitan city.

Why We Need New Churches

Every church begins its life contextualized for a particular time and place. More often than not a church's dominant culture reflects the cultural norms, artistic forms, language, worldview, and ethos of a certain moment. For inherited churches that have survived over generations, ongoing adaptation is essential if they want to continue to speak faithfully as culture changes. Otherwise, you eventually end up with museums and monuments—which is what we largely find across Europe today—rather than thriving Christian communities. The work of adaptation is hard, however, and it is normal for legacy generations to resist transformation in order to reflect a new generation or population's culture rather than their own. Resistance comes because adaptation involves the reworking or loss of cultural forms the legacy generation finds comfortable and meaningful. This is typical (and understandable!) human behavior. Who likes to give up familiar cultural forms in order to learn unfamiliar ones?

Starting new Christian communities offers the ability to begin with contextualized Christian life and witness without having to take the long journey of cultural renegotiation. The gospel can be embodied in culturally-accessible forms from the get-go for people who may be spiritually curious but wouldn't feel at home in inherited churches. Planting new churches brings to the forefront core missional questions that can be overlooked in inherited churches, such as: What might Christian witness look like specifically in this context, with these neighbors, in order to speak and act in terms and ways they can understand? How might Christian community be embodied to reflect what following Jesus looks like in this historical moment, and to challenge it according to Jesus's way? What essentials do we need to claim, and what non-essentials can we release?

Simply put, the work of faithful contextualization is difficult under any circumstances. Recontextualization is much more difficult because it involves changing the existing organizational culture of a local church. Culture is the most challenging part of an organization to change, much more difficult than statements, policies, or structures.[1] Culture is the often-unspoken set of assumptions about how the world works, how time functions, and what is normal and expected. Those with power in existing churches must make space for those in the emerging culture to reshape the community's life according to different norms. This is a challenging process.

Church planting is historically how the Holy Spirit has formed new Christian communities in different times and places that speak the local language and incarnate the gospel as Good News for specific populations. It is an essential dimension of the mixed ecology—a dimension that has been significantly underemphasized in Western contexts with Christendom legacies. It has long been observed that it is much harder to transform and revitalize an existing congregation to speak to its neighbors than to start a new one contextualized for this purpose. With so many existing churches around, however, most denominations and church systems concentrate the vast majority of their time, energy, and resources on legacy churches rather than on cultivating new forms of Christian community. As understandable as this strategy may be, it is not likely to bear fruit over the long term amidst the dramatic social and cultural changes taking place today. The landscape of church planting is unfamiliar to many legacy church members and leaders.

We highlight some of its contours here and explore critically how church planting fits within the mixed ecology.

Approaches to Church Planting: 20th Century Models

In their book *Starting Missional Churches*, Mark Lau Branson and Nicholas Warnes identify four primary approaches to church planting that dominated the 20th century in the United States.[2] The first of these is Suburban Sprawl, which emerged following World War II. As Americans moved into newly-burgeoning post-war suburbs, denominations purchased a plot of land, hired a pastor, constructed a building, and attracted adherents of that denomination. This worked well with members of the greatest generation, the silent generation, and the Baby Boomers. Institutional loyalty and belonging were valued. Even if church members weren't comfortable talking about God or being overly intentional about their spiritual development, joining voluntary associations was a normal and meaningful way to find connection and meaning. Many women who had taken jobs during the war now found themselves with time to volunteer their leadership and gifts. They brought dynamism and energy to their churches, albeit within the constraints of predominantly patriarchal structures.

The basic organizational logic of the Suburban Sprawl approach to church planting was that of the corporate franchise. Denominational headquarters and regional judicatories served as hubs of a centralized command system, creating and disseminating standardized worship materials, Christian education curricula, policies, and procedures. One could visit a church of one's denomination almost anywhere in the country and have a similar experience in worship or Sunday school. There was much less emphasis on listening first to neighbors, adapting the church's life contextually for particular neighborhoods, or discerning how the Spirit might be at work in specific places. The franchise approach was predominant in mainline denominations in particular, which reached their heights of institutional strength during this period.

As the 20th century progressed into the 1960s and 70s, many churches experienced conflict over social and cultural issues. This led to the second major approach to church planting: Protestant Splitting, or what Tim Keller calls "Defiant Church Planting."[3] As denominations and local churches divided over doctrinal purity and social change, new churches were started. However, these churches tended to bring with them many of the same basic contextual assumptions of the prior church. They were less about discerning the Holy Spirit's leading and contextualizing in relation to neighbors than about maintaining theological integrity and traditional practice. Churches split over members' preferences, whether it be the embrace of progressive social trends or worship styles (traditional versus contemporary).

Branson and Warnes point out how the Western Enlightenment stress on certainty fed into this approach. The Reformation, which unfolded within the context of Christendom in Europe, was in large measure a struggle over what constituted the *true church.* As the Enlightenment emerged in its wake, there was cultural anxiety in the West over where to find truth. Being "right" became more important than being unified or belonging together. This merged with 20th century consumerism to foster the Protestant

Splitting paradigm. Members wanted their church to reflect their preferences and attitudes.

The next approach to emerge in the later 20th century was the Expert Strategies model. In a culture that privileged expertise, technology, innovation, and organizational growth and success, church planting was understood to be the work of experts utilizing the latest techniques. Church planting through much of Christian history has been undertaken by local people called and led by God to plant within neighborhoods and networks in which their authority is primarily based on their spiritual lives and relational trust. The Expert Strategies model professionalizes the work of planting and looks to proven technical approaches to secure success. Leaders are often screened through standardized denominational processes according to objective criteria and trained to follow an industrialized approach to building a team, creating a brand, marketing, and launching a worship service. Consultants and denominational/judicatory officials oversee these efforts with a managerial mindset.

The challenge with the Expert Strategies model is that it doesn't require attending closely to the local context, listening deeply to neighbors, and discerning the Holy Spirit's leading. Church planting can become another consumer marketing project like launching a new chain store location. Neighbors can become objects of technical effort rather than subjects in their own right. God's agency can recede into the background. Planters can come from outside the context, with no relational trust or depth of understanding of life there. Their authority is based on technical expertise rather than on spiritual leadership and contextual knowledge and credibility.

The final model that Branson and Warnes describe is perhaps the most widely familiar: Charismatic Figures. A leader with a big personality brings a vision and gathers people to constitute a new church. These leaders are often gifted as speakers, visionaries, and entrepreneurs. Their personality tends to dominate the new church's life and development. Rather than discerning a shared vision among a founding team or local community, the leader may receive and dictate a vision for others to embrace. How God might be at work in the lives of the neighbors the new church hopes to reach can be less of a priority. The Charismatic Figure approach sometimes integrates elements of the Expert Strategies approach.

There are several drawbacks to this approach, as effective as it can seem when a church is growing. A church built on a personality other than Jesus will always have a shaky (and idolatrous) foundation. Charismatic Figures are often reluctant to share power. Decision-making is often centralized in the founding pastor, which disempowers others. When the founding pastor leaves or retires, leadership transitions can be difficult to navigate at best or devastating to the church at worst. Charismatic leaders can fall prey to abusing their power, as we have sadly seen in numerous high-profile pastor scandals in recent years. These leaders can also build a personal brand that becomes more important than serving the local church, distracting them from the primary ministry there.

God can and does work through all these models, and some have been effective. Yet they tend to reflect aspects of late modern Western culture that are less than helpful for the 21st century church. The kind of standardization and denominational loyalty that underpinned the Suburban Sprawl approach does not work any longer in a diverse society where loyalty to institutions has eroded dramatically. The endless (and ongoing) splitting of Protestant churches has communicated to the wider public a profound disunity in violation of Jesus's prayer in John 17 that his followers may be one as he and the Father are one. Expert strategies reduce church planting to yet another consumer and managerial exercise. The downfall of charismatic figures in scandals has brought deep harm to many people and undermined the church's public credibility.

Nicholas Warnes suggests that we need a post-colonial, post-industrial, and Spirit-focused paradigm for planting churches.[4] What does he mean by this? Within the framework of Christendom, it was easy for churches to see neighbors as "targets" of attraction or acquisition into institutional membership, and thus neighborhoods as spaces of conquest or control. This kind of colonial approach overruns cultural differences and seeks to absorb people into systems that can deny their agency and integrity. It is industrial in that efficient formulas are assumed to work anywhere, anytime, within a predominantly managerial ethos. These approaches eclipse rather than prioritize the Holy Spirit's leading. Church planting within the mixed ecology today is vital, but must proceed on different theological grounds.

Joining God's Life in the Neighborhood

The triune God is active in the world and in the lives of our neighbors. This is an essential starting point for Christian mission and church planting. It is the triune God who has a mission in the world in which the church participates, rather than the church having a mission that we ask God to bless.

We must begin with God's agency and leadership if we are to be faithful. This involves ongoing discernment of the Holy Spirit's leading within the work of contextualization, as the church becomes incarnate in relationship with neighbors in a particular time and place.

Beginning with God and neighbors means an outside-in approach rather than the planting team huddling and coming up with its own vision for a new church apart from deep discernment and careful listening to neighbors. There is a mutuality in the connection with neighbors where we expect God to guide the shaping of the new church through their stories, voices, gifts, and invitations. As Stuart Murray notes, rather than approaching church planting as an exercise in "cloning" an existing church, it is an opportunity to explore fresh ways of incarnating the gospel.[5] This means releasing some Christendom assumptions, such as the idea that church = pastor + program + building.[6] Within the mixed ecology, church planting can and should take many different forms.

Fiona Mayne began Haywood Village Church in Weston-super-Mare in the Somerset area of England after she experienced a personal awakening and deepening of Christian faith at age 40.[7] Haywood Village is a relatively new housing development with no existing church, but Mayne had lived nearby for a number of years and knew a lot of people in the area. Through her relational connections and involvement with local organizations, she kept asking people who lived there what they wanted for the neighborhood, and the answer was always: "somewhere to meet up." With encouragement from a local pastor, Mayne started the Take Five pop-up cafe with some people from other area churches. One afternoon a week, the cafe met in the local school community room, growing to about 100 people participating. They were clear from the start that it was being hosted by Christians, but they kept the focus on building community and friendships. People began to say, "You're all Christians; where's the church in Haywood Village?" Mayne said there wasn't one yet, but if there was, what would they like it to be? The response was like the cafe but with Christian content, a place where people could bring their questions about God and share hospitality.

This led to Tea and Toast Church, initially once a month. People would gather for tea, toast, discussion, and engagement with scripture. Some people wanted to go deeper, which led to a weekly Wednesday night group, Rooted. At Rooted, the group eats together, reads and discusses the Bible, prays, and sometimes sings worship songs. Mayne says, "We do a lot of listening, asking for feedback, and trying not to rush in with lots of plans."[8] Rooted became the basis for what emerged as the new church's leadership team. Haywood Village Church is now organized as its own congregation. They gather around tables in the local school for a cafe-style church every week. The context has a lot of economic and social challenges, and the church includes a lot of what Mayne calls "underdogs"—people with addictions, widows, and those struggling in different ways. Everyone is involved in helping, even if it just means setting up chairs. Some people who come regularly aren't Christian, but they value the community and hospitality as they take initial steps to explore spirituality. Haywood Village Church is working with the developer of the housing estate to build a space with a community cafe downstairs and a floor upstairs with space to rent out to various community groups. Mayne is now ordained, having been trained through an alternative minister pathway in the Church of England.

This story offers an example of the kind of organic, lay-led process that emerges out of deep listening and relationships with neighbors. God worked through a leader God had already placed in this community—Fiona Mayne—who had relational credibility and contextual knowledge. The church was both clear about its Christian identity but also responsive throughout to neighbors' voices. The end product looks different from many inherited churches. The focus is on engaging people in exploring spiritual questions, scripture, and life as disciples of Jesus. The church didn't start with the launch of a big worship service, but rather with practices of hospitality and community.

Resource Churches

Gas Street Church in Birmingham, England started in 2014 when Tim and Rachel Hughes, co-senior pastors, and a team from Holy Trinity Brompton Church, a long-established church in central London, relocated to Birmingham's city center. They began with a small midweek gathering in the Hughes' home and then began to meet on Sundays in a variety of spaces, including a law office boardroom and a comedy club. Eventually they discovered an old industrial building used to manufacture the gas that once powered street lamps in the city, located in the nightclub area. Seizing upon the symbolic resonance with the church's vocation to be a light to the world, they renovated it and began to worship there. Within the first year, another church was planted out of Gas Street Church. Within the first three years,

Gas Street Church grew beyond 700. A decade on, over a third of the adult congregation is comprised of ethnic minorities, and 51 nations are represented. Gas Street Church has gone on to plant two additional churches, including one in the Netherlands.[9]

In the Book of Acts, we find two basic approaches to church planting.[10] The first is an approach such as that taken by Paul and his companions as they traveled around the Mediterranean basin starting new churches. They raised up new leaders in these places and moved on. Some of these leaders in turn (such as Apollos) became planters themselves and started additional communities. The second approach is churches planting churches, where an existing congregation trains and sends a team to another location. In the New Testament context, this was often because the initial church outgrew the home it was meeting in, leading to multiple house churches in a particular place. Rather than one or a couple of apostolic leaders starting a new church, a group from an existing church begins a new community.

The resource church model combines elements of both. Resource churches are city-center churches planted to resource their regions by developing leaders and planting churches that will go on to plant other churches.[11] The resource church model begins with a planting team from another church that commits to living in a new context. Often this means a dozen or more families relocating to a new city or neighborhood, finding new housing and jobs. The focus is on urban centers, particularly those with young populations who aren't currently being reached by any church. The team is either invited into an existing congregation that has dwindled, or like Gas Street Church, finds a public venue in which to launch. When there is an existing congregation, the resource plant seeks to honor the legacy ministry in that place while also offering new forms of worship and ministry that connect with neighbors. Sometimes, this means maintaining a traditional service for a period of time alongside launching a new, more culturally-accessible worship experience.

As of 2020, there were 100 resource churches in the UK spread across almost every diocese (regional church system). The most impactful resource church in the UK is Holy Trinity Brompton, which has planted 35 churches since 1985, which have spawned many granddaughter and great-granddaughter churches. Resource churches tend to bring an intentional focus on marginalized populations and social concerns, as well as neighbors who are often hard to reach, developing ministries that address local needs. These ministries evolve from listening to and loving neighbors, which earns credibility in the local context.

Resource churches are intentionally designed to be leadership development incubators. Each resource church plant team includes a church planting curate (apprentice pastor) who is expected to lead a new plant out of the first plant within a few years. Resource churches have seen a 20-fold increase in attendance. Nearly half (46 percent) of attendees are either new churchgoers or people returning after a long absence. While only 6 percent of active participants in the Church of England nationally are aged 18-29, 30 percent of resource church attendees are.[12] Resource churches are an integral way for the Church of England to live into its strategic commitment to become younger and more diverse.

One Size Doesn't Fit All

There are many different forms of church planting emerging today in various contexts, and they all have a role to play. Many don't fit into traditional boxes—either of inherited church, or of what people often imagine church plants to look like. Some of them are intentionally small, more like fresh expressions (see chapter 4) or microchurches (see chapter 5). Others, like resource churches, involve a significant investment of people and resources from the start and seek to grow quickly.

Where church planting works best, it is a vehicle for making new disciples of Jesus. Disciple making hasn't always been the focus of churches, whether legacy congregations or new plants. Within the framework of Christendom, churches were able to attract a crowd of people willing to attend worship services and to support the institution. But this didn't necessarily translate into learning how to follow Jesus in daily life in today's world. Starting a new church offers the opportunity to create a discipleship-focused culture from the start, rather than having to transform an inherited culture with other priorities and preferences. It also allows churches to reflect the diversity of their contexts in ways that many inherited churches struggle to do.

New City Church of Los Angeles began with calls from neighbors. Kevin Haah was an associate pastor at a Korean church in downtown LA who led a ministry in the Skid Row community called Love LA. This ministry focused on a weekly outdoor worship service for the unhoused. Young Nak Celebration Church, where Haah worked, saw Love LA as an outreach ministry, but the Skid Row residents who participated saw it as their church. Yet there was nothing for those Skid Row neighbors beyond the worship service—no community life, Bible study, pastoral care, or discipleship. One day, Haah received a phone call at the church from a stranger, who asked, "What is your church doing to reach the new residents of downtown?" At the time, downtown LA was rapidly growing, with professionals moving in.

Haah, his wife, and the leadership of his church discerned that he was being called to plant a new church downtown that would combine the Skid Row community and the new professionals. New City Church of LA was born in 2007 with a small group praying together and seeking to embody a kingdom vision of socioeconomic, cultural, and racial diversity. They began public worship in 2008 in a restaurant. When they outgrew that space, they started meeting in a theater.[13] Throughout its life, New City Church has reflected the diversity of its urban context. Racially, the church is comprised of about 20 percent each of Asian American/Pacific Islander, Black/African American, Latino/a/Hispanic, and White participants, with the rest being multiracial. Approximately 40 percent have experienced homelessness at some point, while over half are college graduates. Fifteen percent are LGBTQ.[14] The church intentionally built its leadership structures to include representatives from the various communities present, rather than having one group dominate. New City Church offers an example of the kind of multicultural church the Holy Spirit can create when starting from scratch rather than trying to adapt an existing church.

Opportunities and Risks of Church Planting

As we have been describing, church planting offers the promise of fresh contextualization of the gospel and Christian community in a close and responsive relationship with the Holy Spirit and local neighbors. There is freedom to develop a church culture that speaks the vernacular of the people present in the contemporary environment, and to focus the church around practices of discipleship. Planting forefronts the missionary questions of what church should look and feel like in a particular time and place through a process of discernment and experimentation. The examples of church plants listed in this chapter are difficult to imagine within traditional established congregational structures; each is connecting with neighbors who normally wouldn't connect with church.

Church planting also has some limitations and risks. One is that many approaches to planting focus on a worship service as the primary point of contact with neighbors. This works for people with church backgrounds looking for a church to join. But for people who have no experience of church, it is unlikely they will feel comfortable showing up at worship, no matter how contextualized it may be. In a typical church plant, only 50 percent of attendees at the first "launch" service are there a month later.[15] Stuart Murray points out that prioritizing worship is a Christendom legacy. "Launch" imagery comes from shipbuilding, but in some contexts a public launch may not be the best approach.[16]

Christendom defaults can apply when the presumed outcome of church planting is a nonprofit voluntary association institutional congregation that can afford to pay a staff and have a building. Denominations engaged in church planting in the past several decades have often fallen into the trap of assuming that a professional pastor is required whose compensation should be paid initially by the denomination and then fully by the new church through member donations within a three-year period. They have often operated under the assumption that a new church isn't legitimate until 50, 100, or more people are actively participating (and financially supporting the church and in turn the regional church system). These are Christendom, not New Testament, criteria. New Testament churches were smaller, based in homes, and not led by professional pastors. Many places where Christianity is thriving in the world today inhabit alternative models. The track record for mainline denominations pursuing this approach to church planting is poor, as institutional assumptions are contextualized for 20th century, not 21st century, realities. If the aim of church planting is to reach people who are not yet Christian, it can take longer than hoped for; participants may not be ready to formally join and institutionally support a congregation.

Finally, much church planting growth is actually "recirculation of the saints"—transfer growth, or the reactivation of disengaged Christians.[17] It is great for disconnected Christians to discover churches that help them re-engage their faith and grow as disciples. But this doesn't solve the growing challenge of people with no church background or deep suspicion of institutional churches (sometimes based on experiences of church harm). For those neighbors, simpler, organic, relational, and participatory forms of Christian community and witness in daily life are required.

CHAPTER 4

Fresh Expressions of Church

Wildwood United Methodist Church in Wildwood, Florida was a traditional congregation that had dwindled to a handful of elderly members when Pastors Michael and Jill Beck arrived in 2010. Michael Beck grew up in a nearby church, St. Mark's UMC, and experienced firsthand there the power of a local church loving a child who was raised in challenging circumstances. Yet Wildwood had grown disconnected from its neighbors and unsure of its future. Over the next dozen years, Wildwood experienced transformation by becoming a mixed ecology church. Alongside the traditional worship service, over a dozen fresh expressions were birthed.

One of these was Paws of Praise, led by Larry Gaboury, a church member in his 70s. Larry liked to spend Saturday mornings at a local dog park, where he knew all the regulars. He started Paws of Praise as a simple fresh expression of church in the dog park. The dogs would chase each other, and the adults huddled for a time of prayer, the sharing of a Jesus story, and conversation. Wildwood also started Tattoo Parlor Church in nearby Ocala, which meets in a local tattoo parlor at the invitation of the owner. This has led to some elderly legacy church members getting their first ink! Tattoo Parlor Church includes prayer, discussion of a Bible story, and communion.

Church 3.1, led by Denise Orourke, prays, discusses a Bible story, and runs or walks a 5K (3.1 miles). Burritos and Bibles started in a Moe's Southwestern Grill with a few people from the church who gathered to study scripture together and enjoy burritos and all-you-can-eat chips and salsa. Over time, and with the permission of the owner, it grew to encompass dozens of people gathering and the celebration of communion using tortillas as communion bread.

Many of the people who first connected with Christian faith through these fresh expressions also became connected with Sunday worship at Wildwood UMC through a New Life service that took place alongside the legacy traditional service. Today, Wildwood UMC is part of a cluster of three churches overseen by Michael and Jill Beck, including St. Mark's UMC in Ocala and Compassion Church, a new plant in a formerly closed church building. While there are only two legacy congregation members left at Wildwood, the church now continues and has life through the neighbors who found faith through the fresh expressions.

Fresh expressions of church are "new forms of church that emerge within contemporary culture and engage primarily with people who don't 'go to church.'"[1] Another definition is: "Any venture that works mainly with non-churchgoers and aims to become church."[2] The term covers a range of forms of Christian community contextualized within specific neighborhoods and networks where life plays out. They are an attempt to incarnate church in everyday life, going where people already are, rather than trying to attract people to institutionalized church activities and structures. The focus is on listening to, loving, serving, and blessing a particular group of people as a witness to the gospel of Jesus, with the possibility of church emerging in that community. Michael Moynagh writes, "Whereas the traditional approach to evangelism begins with the current church and asks how people can be encouraged to belong, new contextual churches go to where people are and ask what church should appropriately look like in their context."[3]

The phrase "fresh expressions of church" emerged within the Church of England and the British Methodist Church in the early 2000s as a way to describe a variety of new forms of Christian community that were appearing alongside traditional inherited parish churches as experiments in Christian witness and practice in a post-Christian society. George Lings' extensive 2016 study of fresh expressions in the UK lists 20 different kinds: all age worship, alternative worship, base ecclesial community, cafe church, cell church, children-focused church, cluster church, community development plant, intentional community, Messy Church, midweek service, multiple Sunday congregation, network church, new monastic community, new traditional service, older people's church, school-based church, special interest group, church plant, under 5s church, and youth church.[4] Even within fresh expressions themselves there is a mixed ecology! This is by design.

Fresh expressions have four primary characteristics. They are *missional* in that they intend to work with non-churchgoers. They are *contextual* in that they find culturally appropriate ways of reaching people. They are *formational* in that they aim to form disciples of Jesus. They are *ecclesial* in that they provide a taste of church for people who are involved and seek to become church.[5]

Michael Moynagh notes, "Traditionally, Christians have asked what would work well for them and agreed on the time, length, style, and place of their Sunday worship on that basis. Then they have invited others. But the invitation has always been to 'join us' on 'our' terms."[6] Yet the kingdom or reign of God is bigger than just drawing people into the church. It touches on all of life in creation, including life in local neighborhoods and networks outside organized "church" activities.

This renewed understanding of the kingdom and of the triune God's mission in the world undergirds the shift from a "come to us" to a "go together" approach. Rather than organized, episodic "outreach" service programs as the basic unit of mission, fresh expressions are a way for small teams of believers to invest relationship, presence, and love with their neighbors as a form of witness and service. Nothing is forced, because leaders assume that God is already at work in neighbors' lives; they just need to listen for the Holy Spirit's invitation. Moynagh writes, "Just as you might share a stick of French bread with someone by breaking a piece off, so the church breaks off a piece of itself and offers it to others as a new expression of church."[7] These communities are far more accessible to neighbors than traditional churches because they emerge where life is already happening in local areas.

The Fresh Expressions Journey

Hot Chocolate started in 2001 in Dundee, Scotland when a small group of volunteers went out to meet some of the young people who were hanging out on the grass outside Steeple

Church in the city center. Their only agenda was to meet the young people and hear their stories. The young neighbors started calling the encounters "Hot Chocolate" because that is what the Christians offered them along with a listening ear (it was November). Many of these youth came from disadvantaged backgrounds. Relationships began to form, and as they did, the church folks asked the youth, "If you had a wee bit of space in this building, what would you want to use it for?" The young people asked for rehearsal space for their bands and a place to hang out. As they got to know each other, the young adults and church members began to form a community and explore spiritual questions. They gathered around a dinner table and worshiped in ways that responded to the young people and the Spirit's leading. There are now mentors at Hot Chocolate who started as young participants and are passing the community's life on to a new generation. Hot Chocolate now offers a variety of ministries for youth ages 12-21 in Dundee, including art and chat groups, community meals, sports, music, and one-on-one support around a variety of life challenges.[8]

The fresh expressions journey starts differently than a traditional church planting approach, which focuses on preparing for and launching a new worship service, followed by courses or small groups that seek to make disciples of the people attracted to the worship experience. Instead, fresh expressions usually begin with listening to neighbors in spaces where neighbors already spend time, whether that be a cafe, pub, sideline at a youth sports practice, yoga studio, school, or a community center. Out of this listening, small teams of Christians identify hungers, yearnings, and struggles that can be addressed with acts of loving service.

For instance, if people are hungry, the Christians might offer a meal. If people are lonely, they might offer an activity or space to gather and connect for friendship. Out of the listening and loving, community begins to form. The next step is to explore discipleship through opening up conversations about spiritual questions or providing invitations to join a simple spiritual practice (like lighting a candle and praying, or sharing a story from scripture). As people go deeper on this journey, church begins to take shape through regular rhythms of gathering and practice. Eventually, leaders from within the community start the cycle over with new neighbors in other spaces.[9] The journey looks like this:

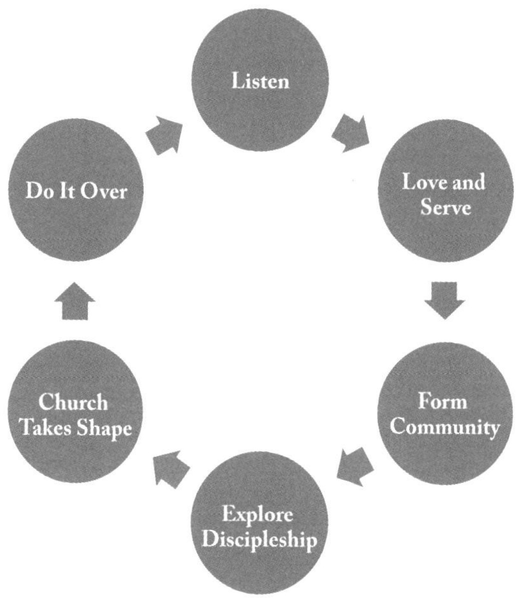

This approach, sometimes known as the "loving first" or "serving first" journey, makes several assumptions. First, the church needs to listen to neighbors in their spaces with a posture of openness (not church-controlled spaces) rather than assume it knows what they are looking for. Such listening, when done with genuine compassion and curiosity and without judging or shaming, can itself be a powerful act of ministry. Second, loving people by addressing their felt struggles and needs models Jesus's way and is essential to building credibility and trust. Much of Jesus's ministry involved asking questions of people to hear their stories and then addressing their struggles through healing, providing food (such as the feeding of the 5,000) or even wine at a wedding party in Cana (thus sparing the hosts the shame of running out), and restoring isolated individuals to community. These steps can take time—sometimes months or even years before enough relational trust is built to engage more explicitly around spirituality. If listening or loving is as far as the journey goes, it is still worthwhile.

Forming community is a powerful way to give people an experience of belonging in a time when so many people are experiencing isolation and loneliness. These steps are all embodied expressions of the gospel—listening, loving service, and community. The step of exploring discipleship explicitly often begins by adding a "spiritual extra" to an outreach activity. This could initially be lighting a candle and having a silent prayer or meditation time. Fresh expressions often include the sharing of a "Jesus story," where someone from the group briefly retells in their own words a story from the Gospels and why they chose it. Listeners are then invited to respond in discussion. Fresh expressions tend to be highly dialogical, encouraging people to speak up, ask questions, share their own perspectives (even if coming from a very different place), and talk back. Going deeper with more intentional worship or spiritual activities takes place when the group is ready or as an option for some within the group.

One of the biblical texts that has inspired the fresh expressions process is Luke 10:1-12, where Jesus sends out the 70 disciples in pairs to prepare people in towns and villages for his coming by sharing the peace, healing the sick, and dwelling with neighbors in their spaces. Jesus directs his followers to travel lightly, without money, baggage, or extra clothing so that they are vulnerable and must depend on neighbors for their well-being. Jesus recognizes the risk of this kind of journey, saying he is sending them out "like lambs into the midst of wolves" (Luke 10:3). The peace they offer won't always be received.

Neighbors who receive sent disciples are known in the fresh expressions movement as "persons of peace." These could be restaurant or business owners who welcome groups to meet in their spaces, people who are well connected and trusted within the community and can open up relationships, or anyone who is open to being a bridge between Christian disciples and the local neighborhood. The journey is one of ongoing discernment and seeking to follow the doors that open, rather than planning ahead of time what will unfold, and on what timeline. Each fresh expression should be contextualized for its particular setting.

Are Fresh Expressions Really "Church"?

Alix Taylor moved from London to Metfield, a small village in the Suffolk area of East England, and had two children at home. She noticed that there was nothing for young people to do in her village. She heard about something called Cook@Chapel for young adults, involving pizza and prayer, and was so excited about the idea she couldn't sleep. The next morning, she set up a meeting with the woman who did all the cooking at church (Taylor didn't like to cook). Eventually Taylor developed an experience for youth with money she received from a local councilor seeking to support community life in the village. It involved cooking, learning, trust and relationship building, and prayer. Many of the children she worked with had never been to church and didn't know the other youth who participated. They were honest, open, and trusted the leaders.

Thus began Cook@Church. The group started off with her two children, quickly grew to 6-7 kids ages 11-13, and then younger siblings wanted to come. Each child had their own work station, ingredients, and equipment in an open environment (like *The Great British Bake Off*). The experience was intergenerational, involving learning basic life skills and sitting down to eat a meal with others. Taylor observes that kids in the area don't often sit around a table or know how to serve others, let others go first, or say a prayer of thanksgiving before they eat. At the end of each session Taylor or another leader would say, "Is there anything you want prayer for next week? Put a piece of paper in the bowl and the leaders will pray for you."

Cook@Church became a way for the large number of elderly residents in the village to come in contact with the younger generation, share stories, and develop friendships. Sylvia, for example, was a pillar of Taylor's traditional church, the backbone of the village. Even though she wasn't on the volunteer schedule, Sylvia would repeatedly show up at Cook@Church sessions with something practical for the participants like a can opener.

She developed a friendship with Taylor's daughter, who was devastated when Sylvia died suddenly.

Throughout this journey, Taylor had the support of her village church. As the idea for this ministry was marinating, Taylor crashed a village committee meeting where members were panicking because they were told the funding they were receiving from the National Lottery needed to be used for something involving young people. Taylor shared her vision and received the funding she needed. As Taylor reflected, "If it hadn't been for the prayers of the village church I would have given up or nobody would have turned up."

Cook@Church is an example of the close relationship between many fresh expressions and inherited churches. The vast majority of fresh expressions are started out of a traditional church, accountable to it, or closely connected. Sometimes, this means sharing leaders, resources, spaces, or participants. Some traditional churches (like Wildwood) launch numerous fresh expressions in their contexts. Some fresh expressions are started by pioneer leaders more independently within a local context, but under the supervision and accountability of a judicatory (regional church system) and its leadership.

One of the questions that has been raised about fresh expressions is whether they constitute "real" church. The answer to that will depend on one's particular ecclesiology (theology of the church). Confessional traditions that emerged during the 16th century Reformation (such as Lutheran and Reformed) tend to assume a Christendom context for the church. They define church as an assembly of believers in which the Word is rightly preached and sacraments administered according to

Christ's ordinances, with some adding the exercise of church discipline. This puts the focus on practices—specifically, clergy doing certain rituals for and with people in a weekly gathering. While proclamation of the Word and sacraments play a role in fresh expressions, there has also been an effort to reframe and expand what constitutes church.

The *Mission-Shaped Church* report of the Church of England identifies four relationships that characterize the church: UP (with God), IN (with each other in fellowship), OUT (with neighbors in witness and service), and OF (part of the whole body of Christ).[10] These four sets of relationships are interlocking and equally important.[11] Fresh expressions have a certain provisional character—they are intentionally experimental and emergent. Michael Moynagh says they are "on the way" to being full church.[12] Some fresh expressions practice baptism and Eucharist, but typically later in the journey of development. Sometimes, participants in fresh expressions will join in the sacramental life of a traditional church, such as for major feast days. This all depends on discernment within the local community, people's readiness to take a next step in faith, and the traditions and practices of the church body connected to the fresh expression.

Leadership in Fresh Expressions

Messy Church was started by Lucy Moore, a lay leader in an Anglican church just outside Portsmouth, England in 2004 as a way to engage young families who weren't otherwise connected to church. It has become the most common form of fresh expression, with over half a million people participating monthly in over 4,000 registered Messy Churches in 30 countries.[13] A typical Messy Church experience begins with a short time of welcome and light refreshments, followed by an all-ages craft time around a biblical theme. After this, participants are invited to a short (15-minute) worship experience contextualized for all ages, often in a separate space (sometimes a church sanctuary). Finally, people gather over a simple hot meal. The whole experience tends to take about two hours, and most Messy Churches meet monthly.

Like Lucy Moore, many leaders of fresh expressions notice a need, step in to experiment, and are encouraged and given permission by their local church to try something new, often without formal leadership credentialing and training. Within the UK, such pioneers have become known as "lay-lay" leaders—those without formal licensing, usually without recognized training, and usually doing this work in their spare time. George Lings found that they make up about a third of all fresh expressions leaders in the Church of England, and they are as effective—if not more—than those with formal training and ordination.[14]

There are three primary roles for fresh expressions—*pioneers*, *permission-givers*, and *supporters*. Pioneers are "People called by God who are the first to see and creatively respond to the Holy Spirit's initiatives with those outside the church; gathering others around them as they seek to establish a new contextual Christian community."[15] Permission-givers are ecclesial authorities like pastors, bishops, church board leaders, or regional church staff who can authorize and make space for fresh expressions within the larger structures and spaces of the inherited church. Supporters are all those called to walk alongside pioneer leaders and offer their prayers, participation, financial support, or other resources to help a fresh expression come to life.

Michael Moynagh explains how the traditional approach to leadership development, in which church leaders are selected, trained, and then deployed, doesn't necessarily work when it isn't clear what kind of community will emerge. Instead, a better alternative is to encourage, recognize, and support the leaders the Spirit is working through in a particular context.[16] Rather than lifting leaders out of their contexts for standardized training so that they can be placed in another context when they finish, developing pioneer leaders often means coming alongside them as they are doing the work and equipping them where they are. As we explore more in chapter 8, leadership development for the mixed ecology must include a variety of approaches, pathways, and modes of education and support.

Research in the UK by an independent research firm has discovered that starting or participating in a fresh expression leads to spiritual growth. For instance, the number of people who reported feeling spiritually alive nearly doubled through participating in a fresh expression, and 86 percent of respondents agreed that the fresh expression had improved their relationship with God. People also reported feeling greater peace, self-worth, and a deeper sense of belonging.[17] One of the fascinating learnings from the British context is that pioneering a fresh expression is usually a pathway to strong growth in discipleship.

Opportunities and Risks of Fresh Expressions

Fresh expressions are learning playgrounds on the edges of the church's life. They have proven effective at connecting with neighbors for whom traditional church is inaccessible, intimidating, or otherwise inhospitable. They inhabit boundary spaces within local neighborhoods and networks where life is being lived out already and people are seeking some measure of meaning, community, and belonging. Fresh expressions assume that God is active in these neighborhood spaces. Mission is about joining in, listening deeply, finding contextualized ways to love people, and when trust and community is built or deepened, inviting people to discover the difference Jesus might make to their struggles, longings, and dreams. They offer tangible experiences of Christian community that can grow into more mature versions of church over time. Moynagh describes them as "foretastes of the kingdom of God."[18]

In a missionary context such as the Western church finds itself in at the moment, these kinds of simple, grassroots experiments in forming Christian community with neighbors in their spaces are integral ways to learn. The long legacy of Christendom has shaped the culture of traditional churches to expect people to show up at predetermined times chosen by legacy church members and leaders, in spaces that may be highly unfamiliar (and threatening) to neighbors, for activities that may make little sense (at least initially). Fresh expressions get the church out of these boxes and into the neighborhood. Along the way, the church must confront questions that go deeper than how to keep the building open and current membership satisfied. The challenge of engaging a culture that has rejected Christianity with the gospel is hard to deny or avoid. This is critical exploration the church must do in our time. As Michael Moynagh puts it, fresh expressions and other new worshiping communities give long-term churches a future.[19]

Fresh expressions also have their limitations and risks. Focusing narrowly on specific populations can result in de facto forms of socioeconomic and cultural segregation, rather than the mixing of generations and cultures that is a critical part of the gospel and God's kingdom. A skateboarder church, for instance, must come to see itself as part of the larger body of Christ so its members can experience God's reconciliation across lines of difference rather than just an embrace of their own particular subcultural community. We must acknowledge, at the same time, that many inherited forms of church are socioeconomically, generationally, or culturally segregated as well. Moynagh writes, "The church must splinter in response to the splintering of society. Only then can it be a source of unity in the world. It must join the social fragments to join the fragments up."[20] The "joining up" of the fragments is key.

While disciple making should be an essential part of fresh expressions, the depth to which fresh expressions focus on and accomplish this is varied. (Again, the same is the case with inherited congregations.) George Lings' study found that 80 percent of Church of England fresh expressions communities were taking intentional steps to grow disciples of Jesus, but 20 percent were not doing so.[21] Without this, they can be experiences of loving community, but not really church. Fresh expressions may not offer as many pathways and resources for people to grow in their walk with Jesus over time as inherited congregations. People can outgrow them as they mature in faith.

Fresh expressions are still fairly new, even as they are rooted in ancient precedents of various forms of indigenous local Christian communities and microchurches. Many face real limitations in the extent to which they will pass their lives on over time. For instance, a fresh expression formed among parents of a particular age group of children around a sport or school will have to adapt when the children grow up and graduate or move on to a different phase of life. This kind of organic evolution or seasonal lifecycle makes fresh expressions more provisional (or seasonal) and less enduring than traditional congregations that have figured out how to serve multiple generations over decades, if not hundreds of years.

One way to think about fresh expressions is that they are organized but organic ways to love neighbors and introduce them to Jesus. Michael Moynagh observes that the journey of developing a fresh expression increases the capacity to love among those who take it. It unleashes new energy and possibility in inherited church systems that have grown disconnected from their neighbors and focused primarily on institutional survival.[22] These are all reasons why fresh expressions play a vital role in the mixed ecology.

CHAPTER 5

Megachurches and Microchurches

Lutheran Church of Hope in West Des Moines, Iowa was formed in 1993 when Pastor Mike Housholder and 20 people started worship in an office suite. Grounded in solid Lutheran theology (in its pietistic expression), the church began to grow quickly. Within several years, they outgrew a series of spaces before constructing a worship center in 2011 with 2,500 seats and a 300-seat chapel. In 2006, the first of numerous satellite sites was launched. In 2020, Hope was approached by Elim Christian Fellowship, a historically Black congregation, about merging. Hope+Elim, the resulting multicultural congregation, was formed in 2021 and worships in a renovated historic church building near Drake University, which now also houses multiple community outreach ministries and a charter school.

Hope's satellite campuses largely feature local preachers rather than a livestream from the main campus in West Des Moines. The Des Moines area is itself growing rapidly in population, and Hope has intentionally sought to be present in areas where new people are moving in. While traditional worship with an organ is offered in the chapel, the primary worship experience at Hope is contemporary, with 40-minute teaching-series sermons that delve into scripture and connect faith to daily life, utilizing a creative pedagogy with video and visuals. As with any megachurch, an array of ministries is offered for all ages, and the church is engaged in extensive community service, both locally and beyond. Hope was named America's fastest growing church in 2022 by *Outreach* Magazine.[1] With around 10,500 in average weekly attendance, it is by far the largest Lutheran congregation in America.

In 2015, a group of people in Forest City, Iowa (about 2.5 hours away from West Des Moines) started gathering in a local community center to watch the Hope livestream and worship together. Eventually, they reached out to Mark Brandt, Hope's online pastor, who offered encouragement. This became Hope's first "local site"—an expression of Lutheran Church of Hope that is lay-led and meets in a community space. (This is different from the satellite campuses, which have buildings and staff and are geographically closer to West Des Moines.) Over time, ten other local sites emerged, as far away as Kansas City and Omaha. They grew from clusters of people in those communities who were already connected to Hope through online worship. These groups formed communities including fellowship, local mission, and mutual care.

Lutheran Church of Hope is a mixed ecology church. Its various expressions (including thriving ministries with college students at Iowa State University in Ames and the University of Iowa in Iowa City) are reaching a wide range of people in the central Midwest. Hope utilizes a highly professional and efficient operational team to provide organizational support to all these forms of church, whether it be finance, human resources, facilities, technology, or curriculum development. The satellite and local sites do not need to replicate these functions independently like many smaller congregations. For the local sites in particular, the planning and execution of worship is provided through the livestream; the Christians gathered in those places can focus on community life, mission and service, and discipleship. The leadership of the local sites is completely volunteer, but they are equipped, coached, and supported by Hope staff. Established congregations without pastors are also reaching out, asking to become Hope local sites.

Why Megachurches Work

Megachurches tend to have a negative reputation in some Christian circles (particularly liberal ones) and in the secular media. There are multiple reasons for this, including high-profile pastor scandals, the embrace of Christian nationalism by certain megachurches in recent years, and assumptions about their theological depth. They can be viewed as the Walmarts of American Christianity, sucking people out of traditional smaller congregations to consolidate them into bigger enterprises with which small churches can't compete. While the median attendance in American congregations has declined dramatically (by 50 percent in the last two decades, from 137 to 65), 71 percent of congregations with membership over 1,500 *increased* in size between 2015 and 2020.[2] Congregational members are being concentrated in fewer, larger churches. Over 50 percent of American churchgoers belong to the largest 10 percent of churches.[3] What constitutes a megachurch, and why are they so popular?

The standard definition of a megachurch is a Protestant congregation with 2,000 or more in average weekend attendance.[4] By this count, there are around 1,750 megachurches in the United States as of 2020—500 more than in 2006.[5] While megachurches aren't new—they have longstanding ecumenical precedents in American Protestantism, such as Marble Collegiate in New York or Angelus Temple in LA—they are an increasingly significant part of the church landscape.

There is no single type of megachurch. Scott Thumma and Dave Travis identify four categories of megachurches: 1) old line/program-based; 2) seeker; 3) charismatic/pastor-focused; and 4) new wave/re-envisioned. The old line/program-based are often large downtown churches such as Trinity United Church of Christ in Chicago or St. Martin's Episcopal Church in Houston. Their worship and programming may be traditional, but they qualify as megachurches by sheer size. Seeker megachurches were pioneered by Willow Creek in Chicago and Saddleback in Orange County, California. They are designed to offer a welcoming experience to spiritual seekers, typically deemphasizing the "churchiness" of their cultural expressions. Charismatic/pastor-focused megachurches revolve around a charismatic leader. Examples include The Potter's House in Dallas (led by Bishop T.D. Jakes) or Lakewood Church in Houston (led by Joel Osteen). New wave/re-envisioned megachurches emerged with younger pastors over the past two decades and often have a more alternative vibe. A more recent example is The Belonging Co., which focuses on the creative community in Nashville.

Nearly two thirds of megachurches belong to a denomination. Ten to twelve percent are predominantly African American, 2 percent mostly Asian, and 2 percent mostly Hispanic.[6] There has been significant growth in the last 20 years in multiracial megachurches (defined as 20 percent or more minority presence), from 21 percent in 2000 to 58 percent in 2020.[7] Studies have shown that the membership of megachurches tends to reflect considerable economic diversity.[8] Megachurches are more likely to serve adults with special needs than smaller churches.[9] Only a quarter of megachurches fit the profile people often imagine—that of a non-denominational, seeker-oriented church embracing capitalism, the Republican Party, and evangelical theology, led by an authoritarian leader.[10]

Megachurches are contextualized for contemporary American society on multiple levels. We live in a time of malls, megastores, and large corporations. At the same time, megachurches recognize and address the individual yearnings and fragmentation of the Age of Authenticity. They make the most of a free market religious economy where people choose to affiliate and disaffiliate based upon personal preference and experience rather than loyalty to denominations. Megachurches provide spaces that are less intimidating for people to show up at than the tightly-knit communities of smaller churches, but then invite people into a journey of connecting and belonging through small groups and serving. They are oriented toward the transformation of the self, which is a primary cultural focus of contemporary American life.

James K. Wellman, Jr., Katie Corcoran, and Kate Stockly suggest that megachurches address six core desires:

> The genius of these churches, whether always intended or not, was to respond to and meet the deepest needs of their attendees with 1) a spirit of welcome, 2) a deep sense of joy, 3) inspiration from the leader, 4) the possibility of deliverance from regrets and past patterns, 5) the discovery of one's strengths and the sharing of one's weaknesses in fellowship, and finally, 6) the possibility of using one's gifts to serve those in need.[11]

This happens through the intentional structuring of every aspect of member involvement and participation, as Thumma and Travis note. Unlike smaller congregations, which function more informally, megachurches have well-developed systems to meet newcomers where they are and lead them toward deeper connections. This begins with up-to-date, accessible websites (which are often the only church websites in an area that are actually designed for non-believers rather than insiders). It includes teams of friendly greeters and efficient parking systems, lively and easy-to-sing music, regular new member classes, and invitations to join small groups.[12] People can lurk in the crowd if they want, but then take steps toward deeper involvement when they're ready.

The teaching in megachurches typically uses accessible language and illustrations from popular culture that are familiar to a wide range of people. There is often a clear focus on how to live differently because of the gospel and a practical orientation to faith in daily life. This often means thematic teaching series rather than lectionary-based approaches. Many megachurches have grown around the speaking and teaching gifts of founding pastors, and the message plays a central role. Significant time is invested in the preparation and delivery of 35-45 minutes sermons.

Megachurches utilize the strength of their numbers and resources to engage extensively in community service activities. These include support groups, feeding and housing initiatives, substance abuse and twelve-step programs, thrift stores, and other social ministries. According to the Faith Communities Today survey, megachurches were slightly more likely to agree strongly that they were working on social justice than the broader range of American congregations.[13]

These service ministries come out of a culture that combines an open, accessible welcome with an invitation to high commitment. Following Jesus is understood to be transformational. Through small groups, people experience intimate community, often at a more vulnerable and explicitly spiritual level than small congregations, where people know each other well but don't necessarily share their spiritual struggles and journeys directly. People in megachurches know as many or more people at their church than people in smaller churches. Studies have found megachurch members feel a strong sense of belonging.[14]

Throughout, megachurches embrace values of professionalism and operational excellence. There are armies of volunteers helping to run megachurches, but the core institutional maintenance is handled by staff. This is different from many smaller churches, where the church's primary ask of people is to help maintain the institution through serving on committees or taking care of the property. The primary ask in megachurches is often transformation of the self and one's life, which includes participation and serving in the church. One major difference is that serving in the megachurch is often an outgrowth of personal transformation, which is the main focus, rather than a way to move toward it. This meshes much better with the present cultural moment. Even though megachurches are technically voluntary associations (writ large), they are far more tailored to the desires and needs of the Age of Authenticity.

Opportunities and Risks of Megachurches

Some of the things that make megachurches so compelling and effective can also have downsides. Charismatic leaders can abuse their power. The list of megachurch pastors brought down by scandal is sobering. However, there is no evidence showing that megachurches are more prone to scandal than smaller churches. They tend to receive more publicity when it happens, and the fallout can be greater because of their size in a community.[15] Megachurches can uncritically embody aspects of consumer and entertainment culture. The hype and show can be attractive, but also deeply in tension with a crucified messiah whose way was about simplicity and sacrifice. Creating and maintaining the complex system of a megachurch's operations and programming can be exhausting to pastors, staff, and volunteers. Organizational success (as measured through attendance and resources) can become the primary goal, rather than new life in Christ.

Theologically, megachurches are a mixed bag. Megachurches built around a prosperity gospel may draw crowds but disappoint when people experience suffering rather than the material blessings they are promised.[16] Riches of the Christian tradition, such as liturgy, sacramental life, and contemplative prayer, may be underutilized or neglected.

One of the most common criticisms of megachurches is about their political engagement, which is often assumed to be right-wing. There are visible examples, such as Pastor Robert Jeffress of First Baptist Church in Dallas embracing Donald Trump and Christian nationalism.[17] Yet a closer look at the megachurch landscape reveals that less than 20 percent of megachurches engage in direct political activities (and some of those who do are on the political left). One of the main reasons for this is that politics is divisive, and megachurches want to welcome and include as many people as possible.[18] Many megachurches carefully avoid political pronouncements and function as purple zones in an America polarized between red and blue.

Overall, we think megachurches play a vital role in the mixed ecology. They are far more accessible than many smaller and traditional churches to people unfamiliar with Christian faith. They focus on life transformation through the gospel and mix populations in ways many smaller churches don't. They connect faith and daily life when many congregations don't know how to (or don't really care to). They can harness the resources and strength of multitudes to serve neighbors. They help people discern and utilize their spiritual gifts to love others. In an increasingly lonely society, they connect people into small groups to experience belonging.

Megachurches aren't for everyone. Not all people will feel welcome or at home in them. Not all will resonate with the theology at many megachurches or feel like the worship and music speak to them. Some look at the vast energy and resources required to sustain these forms of church and intentionally choose a simpler way. Others have had experiences of spiritual abuse or seen the impact of scandals at megachurches and don't want to go back. At a time when some people in society are eschewing large corporate entities and manufactured experiences for local, craft products and ways of life, the megachurch may not be a good fit. While megachurches have the power to be influential and transformational for large numbers of people in their communities, some Christians are intentionally seeking an opposite approach to influence and transformation by treasuring the small.

Microchurches

A number of years ago, Hugh Halter and Taylor McCall moved with their families to Alton, Illinois, a socioeconomically struggling town just by the Mississippi where Halter's son lived in a care facility for adults with severe epilepsy. Both had earlier been involved in experiments in contextualizing the church in neighborhood spaces through local, organic relationships with neighbors in other cities. Through prayer and discernment, their families felt God was calling them to Alton. They began by simply being present, listening, and forming connections with people as they paid attention to God's leading. Over time, opportunities began to open up. For McCall, it was engaging with youth on his block around basketball, together with his own children. When a tree in McCall's backyard blew over in a storm, crushing his garage, he used the opportunity to replace it with a basketball court for the neighborhood. A nearby park had recently been the location of a shooting, and neighborhood parents and grandparents weren't letting their children play there anymore. McCall's backyard basketball court became a new hub of activity.

The post office in downtown Alton had been boarded up for 60 years. Over time, the man who owned the building offered it to Halter, sensing that he and other Christians would know what to do with it on behalf of the larger community. Eventually, this became Post Commons, a cafe and event space. The city lacked any kind of central public gathering space, and Post Commons became the new community hub—a space where people would work, meet, and form relationships. Halter met a young woman in recovery who wanted to open a bakery but lacked the resources to do so. She was invited to use the commercial kitchen in the Post Commons and sell her pastries there. She and her partner were deeply skeptical of Christians, but as the Post Commons leaders sacrificially let her keep a greater percentage of the proceeds from her pastries and eventually save enough to open her own storefront bakery, they acknowledged it was hard to keep hating Christians.

The Alton Christian community members all live in the city and gather weekly around tables in their homes (or in the Post Commons) to break bread, pray, share life, and welcome neighbors. This community is a kingdom-focused microchurch. Its members are embedded in the neighborhood. Its worship is distributed in smaller gatherings. It intentionally seeks to share its resources with neighbors for their economic empowerment and justice. It has missional businesses (like the Post Commons) that provide economic investment in the city. Members of the community aren't paying for church staff or dedicated church buildings. They focus on Christian practices interwoven into life with an intentional call to seek the flourishing and peace of the city (Jeremiah 29:7).[19]

If megachurches are the supersized, expensive, programmatic, professionally-led versions of church increasingly prominent in contemporary America, microchurches are the opposite. The microchurch movement has emerged in the past few decades as an alternative form of Christian community, sometimes populated by people who have fallen (or been pushed) out of bigger forms of church and who are seeking a simpler, more grounded way of following Jesus. McCall and Halter liken them to the ancient Christian catacombs in Rome—"a refuge for people to find when all else has let them down."[20] Some microchurch participants and leaders have been burned or burned out by their involvement in other forms of church or simply can't square what they find in the Gospels with their experience of much of American Christianity.

While microchurches were the original form of New Testament church and have found expression throughout Christian history (see chapter 2), the contemporary American microchurch movement emerged out of Tampa, Florida in the early 2000s. Brian Sanders was a campus ministry worker at the University of South Florida who cultivated student communities focused on simple Christian practices and relationships with the poor. He found that when students graduated, they were deeply frustrated by not being able to find a church that reflected the authentic depth of spiritual engagement and justice orientation they had known as students.

This led to experiments forming small communities—microchurches—that gathered in homes and community spaces around scripture, prayer, shared life, and relational service with neighbors who were struggling with addiction, poverty, or other challenges in urban Tampa. Participants recognized they had much to unlearn from their prior experiences of middle-class church. A group moved to the slums of Quezon City in the Philippines for nine months to live among the poor and learn from church leaders who ministered there. During that time, a vision began to emerge that was put into practice back in Tampa when they returned.

Sanders and his community asked what the essential minimum is to have church. They settled on three things: *worship* (being in consistent, devoted relationship with Jesus Christ), *community* (being accountable and connected to each other), and *mission* (making disciples and proclaiming the Good News of the kingdom of God).[21] This simplified ecclesiology seeks to reverse the way many churches function, where 20 percent of staff and volunteers provide religious experiences to the other 80 percent, who consume them largely as spectators.[22] In the microchurch world, ordinary church members are understood to be missionaries. Everyone owns the practice and sharing of their faith.

Microchurches tend to be neighborhood-based and develop organically, often slowly. A family or a few Christians will prayerfully develop relationships of trust with neighbors in a particular context. Over time, when spiritual questions and conversations naturally arise, microchurch missionaries will share aspects of their own spiritual stories and invite further discussion and exploration. For those neighbors interested in learning more about Jesus, simple Bible study is made available through methods like Discovery Bible Study.[23] Over time, an extended "spiritual family" or microchurch may emerge, gathering in homes or local community spaces.

The microchurch structure is itself simply a vehicle for making disciples of people who otherwise wouldn't engage with a traditional church. Sanders notes the current collapse of old forms of church, particularly now following the COVID-19 pandemic, where so many people are simply not returning. Rather than try to remedy this with some version of heroic leadership or organizational success, we need to rediscover the basics: "If we cannot be the church in its simplest form, then we cannot be the church in a more complex form."[24] He goes on to question the whole consumer model of church that predominates American Christianity: "We have made a Faustian deal with the devil trading the power of God (his strength) for a flawless church service. And we have lost our soul in the process."[25]

Microchurches have an ethos of humility, sustainability, patience, and emergence as grassroots leaders practice their own rhythms of life as disciples and invite their neighbors who are curious and open to learning more about Christian faith to do so. This doesn't require buildings, budgets, professional clergy, or all the trappings of institutional church. Microchurches are reproducible—any disciple can lead one where they are. Sanders writes, "The microchurch is uniquely equipped to go anywhere.

It is easy to start, easy to lead, and always contextualized."[26] Each microchurch will look different based on the local setting and community. Because microchurches are institutionally light, they can easily be adapted. This is different from the franchise mentality of many American churches and denominations over the past 75 years.

Leadership and Structure in Microchurches

As observed earlier in this book, we live in an age of networks. Hierarchical bureaucracies are being supplanted by network organizations as a more distributed, flexible way of relating and accomplishing things. Microchurches should not exist in isolation (which is risky and problematic on multiple levels) but in networks of support, equipping, and accountability.[27] Tampa Underground is one such network that links over 100 microchurches into one structure. The microchurches are autonomous but united by their agreement to a shared set of values and standards of character and conduct. The Underground organization functions as a mission agency whose sole purpose is to provide a service platform for microchurches to be planted, equipped, supported, and stimulated to grow and thrive.[28] There is a governing structure in which each microchurch is overseen by a body of elders. These elders are in turn accountable to a group of governing elders who are some of the most respected members of the larger body of microchurch elders. They monitor and maintain the values and standards agreed to by the whole body. They approve the ordination of new elders, and discipline or remove elders in case of misconduct or moral failing. They function as overseers.

At the same time, the Underground functions as a nonprofit mission organization with a board of directors, an executive director, staff, and programs. These are all aimed to resource the local microchurches with training, financial services (donation processing, tax, and basic human resources), media services (logo and web design, video and print media), facilities (printing services, classrooms, free clinic, and co-op spaces for meetings and co-working), and coaching (every microchurch is assigned a trained coach). In this way the Underground is both a movement and an architecture. Resources are shared, but more efficiently than the traditional congregational structure, where many of these functions are duplicated in adjacent churches. There are paid staff in the mission organization, but most of the microchurch elders are not paid. They have other jobs or sources of income.

In the "Brave Cities" approach to microchurches described by Hugh Halter and Tyler McCall, the business model is radically different from traditional congregations. These microchurches develop a mixture of benevolent businesses (which are economically self-sustaining and aimed at addressing community needs), justice works, and intentional homes. The aim is to create economic flourishing in an area, not spend the church's resources primarily on church leaders and buildings. The businesses are themselves an expression of mission. They are not charity, but sustainable ways to provide livelihoods for struggling neighbors and bring about economic empowerment. Halter and McCall write, "Though we don't use the term often, we see 'church' as simply the group of people connected to and caring for the city they live in as they share, invest, and leverage all their combined assets to experience and extend the shalom of God to anyone they can."[29]

Opportunities and Risks of Microchurches

As with megachurches, microchurches may not be for everyone. On the one hand, they bring a clarity of focus on disciple making that is rare in traditional churches. Everyone takes ownership of following Jesus and growing into a Jesus-shaped life in relationship with neighbors in a culture and structure of mutual empowerment. They are institutionally much more streamlined and sustainable than expensive forms of traditional church. Resources are shared with neighbors in need rather than consumed by church staff and buildings. Microchurches are rediscovering essential elements of what it means to be church that have been lost or neglected. They are leading the way for the broader church to "go back to basics" in a post-Christendom era.

Microchurches also involve a very different kind of social contract or set of expectations than traditional churches. For people shaped by traditional church, the kind of disciple making and missional practices that are normal within microchurches will be a real stretch. A lot of intentional formation would be required for them to shift into this mode should they choose to embrace it. Many microchurches are relatively new, have emerged within non-denominational evangelicalism, and haven't demonstrated intergenerational longevity, which is one of the gifts of inherited churches. It isn't clear how widely this movement will spread and how long it will last.

Microchurch leaders are not typically educated formally in theology. This may be a blessing in some ways (formal theological education can separate people from neighbors and diminish people's ability to speak about their faith in language that makes sense to others). It can also be a liability if the theological depth of the microchurch's life isn't deep enough to sustain doubts, questions, and growth over time. The professionalized/clerical model of theological education has all kinds of problems, but it does give leaders access to a grounding in the richness of Christian thought over the centuries that can be a vital well to draw on over the seasons of a community's life. Sacraments in the microchurch are more informal and organic (sharing Eucharist over tables at home, for instance, rather than in a formal liturgy). Depending on your particular tradition, this can be a gift and also a limitation. Microchurches are a promising sign of how some Christians are rediscovering how to be church in a post-Christendom society. The humility of these communities is something every Christian community could learn from.

CHAPTER 6

Digital Church

We met Diamond at an event in downtown Minneapolis. She is a mom with five children who considers herself a Christian believer but can't find a church where she feels like she fits in or that is accessible for her schedule. As an African American in Minnesota, Diamond has limited options for churches that are culturally contextualized for her, and she works on Sundays. While she doesn't belong to a congregation or attend worship in person, Diamond avidly watches a bishop from across the country preach on YouTube each week. She finds spiritual nourishment and encouragement through this digital experience.

Dawnlynn is a massage therapist who owns her own business in a suburb of St. Paul. She is a single mother of three teenagers, one of them adopted through the foster care system. Dawnlynn grew up in rural Minnesota in a family that struggled financially, fought constantly, and were, in her words, "dysfunctional." Many of Dawnlynn's high school classmates have died from opioid addiction. Thanks to Dawnlynn's maternal grandparents, who were Christian and important spiritual and personal mentors, Dawnlynn believed Jesus could help her change her life and discover a hopeful future. She started listening to podcasts that helped her rethink and retool her priorities, habits, and lifestyle. She longed to be part of a church community, but like so many

Americans, had to work on Sundays. Thankfully, Dawnlynn found a church on Facebook that included sermons, Bible studies, a chance to interact with other Christians, and a sense of community. While she desired to be part of an in-person faith community, Facebook church sustained her until she was in a place where she and her children could attend church in person.

Diamond and Dawnlynn's stories are not unusual. The COVID-19 pandemic forced Christian churches across the spectrum to experiment with digital church. For some, it remains a primary way of connecting with Christian community. Some congregations were well positioned when lockdowns began in their technological capabilities, culture, and practices. Others found themselves scrambling. Many ministries are now hybrid, including in-person and digital elements and communities. There are still people reluctant to rejoin in-person worship for various reasons, including health or mobility challenges. Others joined churches in different geographic areas and continue to engage with them online. Many congregational leaders struggled to adapt to doing church digitally and were happy to stop when the pandemic ended. Others continue to offer hybrid worship and programming. Some churches only exist in the digital space.

Digital church raises all kinds of questions of what it means to be the body of Christ in a culture increasingly defined by digital technology. What does it mean to participate and belong online? Is digital church "real" church? What about sacraments? While this chapter cannot give digital church the full treatment it deserves, we explore some of the ways in which contextualizing Christian community within online spaces is a necessary part of the mixed ecology. As with other expressions of church already discussed, digital church also has opportunities and risks.

Migrating Online

Washington National Cathedral overhauled its cameras and media setup in 2019. As an institution used to hosting televised events, it was well positioned when the pandemic struck. For Episcopalians and others who wanted a formal liturgical experience that was no longer accessible in their local parish church, Washington National Cathedral became a natural place to turn. At the peak of COVID-19, 5,000 people regularly joined the livestream each week. About 120 people would also engage in coffee hour on Zoom. As of this writing, several thousand still join weekly to watch the worship livestream. They come from up to 30 states and 37 countries. The cathedral recently hired a digital pastor, Jo Owens, who leads online support groups and book studies in Advent and Lent and does Zoom coffee chats with people. The audience is primarily older white Episcopalians, many of whom also have a local parish church they attend in person. The beauty and sophistication of the cathedral's worship, music, and preaching draws them online.

On another side of the ecclesial spectrum is Life.Church, an Evangelical Covenant congregation started in Oklahoma by Pastor Craig Groeschel and his wife Amy in 1996. Life. Church now engages over 90,000 people in person each week at 45 campuses in 12 states and reaches over 140,000 each week virtually in over 130 online services.[1] With 17 million social media followers, Life.Church has long been a pioneer in digital church, including launching the free YouVersion Bible app.

Life.Church records services on weekends and replays them throughout the week with live digital pastors who engage viewers interactively in the chat. These pastors invite prayers through the chat and encourage online viewers to take deeper steps of connection. While Life.Church started in Oklahoma and has campuses primarily in the South-Central United States, the church's preaching is aimed at a national audience. Like many multi-site megachurches, the message at Life.Church's many campuses is delivered by video or sometimes by a local pastor. Some people gather for watch parties of the online services in homes or other local neighborhood spaces. Life.Church makes its content available for free, including small group and children's and youth materials.

These two churches are each in their own way seeking to open up their life to those who aren't physically nearby, can't attend weekend services, or who aren't ready to show up at worship in person. They are using their considerable resources to produce a high-quality worship experience (in terms of music, preaching, and the arts) that most local churches can't match. Both are grounded in physical community life but also use technology to make that life at least partially accessible to those not in person. It is striking to note that Life.Church continues to open satellite campuses across the country to multiply access to physical locations. Online does not replace in-person in the life of these churches, but complements it.

As we think about digital church, it is vital to recognize that imagining a stark binary between digital and physical is unhelpful. Keith Anderson explains: "The choice between digital and face-to-face is ultimately a false one in part, because . . . it defies people's lived experience. Our daily lives are often far more integrated—and digitally integrated—than religious leaders or institutions perceive."[2] Digital technology allows for connections. Our physical and virtual worlds often overlap and can be continuous.[3] Think about the relationships in our lives that have both physical and digital dimensions, such as texting a family member or friend you will see later that day. In a world in which digital technology is interwoven into so many aspects of our lives, digital and physical functionally often overlap, and most expressions of digital church are hybrid. Most American congregations now have some kind of online presence, livestreamed worship, digital access to sermons, or other media. This is seen as an essential part of ministry in today's culture.

Contextualization within Digital Culture

The digital space is best thought of as its own kind of cultural context. How we show up, interact, create, collaborate, and behave in digital spaces is different from physical-only spaces and from traditional cultures. While religious identity was at one time primarily defined by family and community, in Western cultures it is now fluid and constructed by individuals as a lifelong project. Rather than submit to traditions passed down over the generations and mediated by religious authorities, people seek to choose their own path and assemble their own religious and spiritual identities, beliefs, and practices.[4] There is less concern for the coherence of religious identity and submission to traditional authorities than there is for a personal sense of what feels right or fits into preexisting cultural frameworks.

Jeffrey Mahan observes that digital culture is characterized by *hyphenation*, *sampling*, and *mashup*. Hyphenation is the linking of two distinct traditions, such as those who claim to be Christian-Buddhist (how the profoundly divergent theological and cosmological visions of these two faiths cohere is of less concern). People feel free to join elements of disparate traditions together to form a hybrid identity, sometimes at a relatively superficial level. Sampling is a term that comes from hip hop music, whereby pieces of earlier songs are incorporated into a new song. People do the same with religious beliefs and practices, either within one religious tradition or across traditions. For instance, how many times have you heard Christians invoke the term "karma" (a concept at odds with basic Christian teachings about grace)? Mashup is another musical term describing people's combining of elements of different traditions without a clear home base in any single tradition. The individual self is at the center, not one tradition or community.[5]

Digital culture is also a culture of consumption.[6] While consumption of religious experiences and resources is not new, digital culture shapes people to have a basic relationship with media as takers and buyers, seeking to be entertained, with the ability to switch channels (websites, livestreams, podcasts, videos, etc.) at will. Digital culture forms us to expect media to deliver what we want, when we want it 24/7, on-demand. This can lead people to view faith communities as vendors of religious goods and services and faith leaders as simply content creators in a crowded field of digital influencers vying for attention.

At the same time, digital culture is also participatory, where people expect to be able to add their voice, interact, question, collaborate, and co-create rather than just passively consume. While sitting through a traditional in-person church service each week can be highly passive, watching a livestreamed or recorded service in your own living room can relegate Christian worship to a private, individual exercise detached from real interactions with humans in community. The impulse toward participation in digital cultures is fruitful when it involves meaningful interaction and relationship-building. Similar to social activism that only consists of "liking" social media posts, it is easy to keep things superficial and not experience real transformation. The promise of digital engagement is in the collaborative possibilities digital media open up and how seamlessly people can join and contribute.

Dislocation

The digital age is in many ways a dislocated world—a world where place matters less. Geographical context and all that comes with it—history, local culture, and embedded relationships (what the French call *terroir* to denote the unique conditions for producing wine in specific vineyards)—cease to define human interactions in the digital world. Digital spaces have their own cultural features, norms, and expectations that sometimes mirror geographical cultures, and other times transcend or disrupt them. People can find each other across vast distances in ways that would never have been possible otherwise. Relationships and connections can form unhindered by physical proximity.

Stories can be shared that would otherwise be unknown. And, as we all know, the worst of human behavior can be unleashed with little concern for neighbors or accountability, sometimes amplified by algorithms.

Digital media have created an economy of religious and spiritual influence that can be disconnected from the specific realities, concerns, and stories of particular communities. We can all listen to podcasts or video recordings of our favorite preachers from anywhere in the world. The word they preach may be powerful, but its ability to speak concretely to the particular situation of our own local community is limited. The stories and concerns of the people we share life with in local Christian communities will not be heard or addressed in preaching from a church thousands of miles away. The temptation today is to follow celebrity digital gurus of all types rather than invest the time in cultivating local relationships. The digital era renders the local expression of Christian community just one option among many for people to seek and fluidly engage in or disengage from. This breaks the traditional monopoly that local religious leaders have held in influencing their communities, which can be both a bad and good thing.

In the Age of Authenticity, there is the freedom to define one's own relationships and identity. Digital media promise the possibility of doing this with ease and access to endless options. People can try on identities, dip their toe in the water of spiritual communities and traditions without committing deeply, and extract elements from the traditions without concern for their context and how they fit into a whole. At its best, this provides means for people to explore and test out spiritual options they might otherwise not be exposed to. For instance, many people will watch an online service before showing up at a new church in person for the first time. People can hear the gospel of Jesus and encounter Christian community online with low barriers to entry. At its worst, this leads to superficial engagement and lack of depth of relationship with God and other believers.

Networks

Networks have supplanted traditional communities and modern bureaucracies as the primary way of connecting and organizing in digital culture. Networks function differently than traditional local communities, which are characterized by relatively stable relational ties rooted in place, often over generations. Modern bureaucracies arose in the late 19th and early 20th centuries with an industrial economy as ways to organize large systems efficiently. Networks have accompanied the information economy as the primary way people organize and relate. It is important to note that most inherited church structures (local congregations, regional church systems, and denominations) are designed for the traditional local community or bureaucratic eras, not the network era.

Networks are shaped by flows of information and distributed authority. Unlike traditional communities or bureaucracies, where influence and authority are defined by hierarchical position, digital culture provides opportunities for anyone within the network to gain influence from any location. Credentials matter less than perceived authenticity. Agency is shared, and spontaneous collaboration is possible in ways and at a scale that would otherwise be impossible. Relationships are more fluid in networks, and the structure itself tends to be self-organizing rather than imposed from above. Digital networks are not without their own structural forces, for instance in the form of algorithms that shape online interactions, particularly within social media. Digital networks bring empowerment to almost any participant and can threaten the traditional authority of leaders. They can also foster mob behavior, spread untruths, and amplify the most toxic voices and ideas.

Ministry in the Digital Space

Jeff Evans is a youth pastor in Crossville, Tennessee whose passion for the gospel of Jesus and for video games led him to show up in live online gaming platforms like Twitch and Discord as a spiritual presence to the community gathered there. Jeff used his fluency in these digital spaces to establish credibility and invite people to engage with the gospel. At one point, this took the form of preaching within the game Grand Theft Auto, where he secured permission to host a church service in the game's virtual space. This work led to Jeff making videos in which he would reflect theologically on various artifacts and elements in the broader popular culture and share his Christian faith. The videos gained a significant following, particularly among the young men who inhabited these digital communities.

Christian mission has always involved going to where people are. There are many people in today's world who have no relationship with organized religion and have no intention of showing up at an inherited church but who are spiritually open and curious. Many of them spend significant time in digital spaces, whether it be social media platforms, online communities, websites, podcasts, or other venues. The church must go to them. Ministry in digital spaces has to reflect some of the shifts in culture and authority that are taking place.

This begins with a posture of openness to questions and dialogue. If religious authorities expect to have automatic trust and influence by nature of their position or credentials, that is much less the case online. Christians who want to offer a faithful witness and form community in digital spaces will have to begin where people are, invite questions and discussion, and tolerate the ambiguity of the free-for-all that often unfolds there. This doesn't mean Christians should simply affirm and bless whatever people share uncritically. But it does mean they will need to earn a hearing by first listening deeply. Many people in secular culture expect Christians to be judgmental and exclusive. This perception will only change through people experiencing alternative behavior.

Keith Anderson talks about ministry leaders becoming "discoverable"—available for connection with others who might be seeking it (like a Bluetooth device). This might mean being visible and present in online spaces, posting regularly and sharing content that others can find and engage with. Digital ministry involves convening—bringing people together for conversation and community. In this context there is conversation about questions that matter to people where the gospel can be shared. The role of leaders in digital ministry is to facilitate. Anderson frames this as *connecting*, *convening*, and *conversing*.[7]

Digital and Local

Theologian Deanna Thompson was deeply skeptical of digital connections and community until she found herself facing a devastating experience. She was diagnosed with stage IV cancer, suffered a broken back, and was hardly able to move as she endured months of debilitating, isolating treatment. Thompson describes how the digital world enabled connections that were otherwise impossible. This included the use of a CaringBridge page to share updates, reflections, and prayers with people across her life, which led to communities around the world praying for her healing as news spread. Physical visits were impossible or difficult. Virtual connections allowed people to care for Thompson, stay in relationship, express their love, and to walk with her through her harrowing journey.[8]

Digital ministry makes Christian community and connections available for those who can't physically attend. This is an important dimension for the sick, elderly, and disabled, who otherwise might be excluded from church participation. Thompson observes that what sociologists call "weak" and "strong" relational ties applies both to the physical and virtual worlds.[9] We often assume that the digital world is one of weak ties and thin connections. But physical relationships can be similarly weak, while digital ties can be strong and lead to transformational encounters and experiences. Anderson suggests that any digital social media strategy be connected to a local strategy, and vice versa.[10] It is best to think of digital and physical church on a continuum, or as fruitfully overlapping.

On Easter Sunday a couple of years ago, a visitor showed up at Lutheran Church of Hope in West Des Moines, Iowa (the megachurch described in chapter 5). She had flown from Washington, DC, where she lives, for the service. This woman had discovered Hope online and watched their livestream during the COVID-19 pandemic while she struggled through treatment for thyroid cancer. When she was able to travel, she made the trip from DC to Iowa, because she felt moved to join in person the community that had become so significant spiritually to her online. She wanted to be present to celebrate the resurrection with them.

Opportunities and Risks of Digital Church

Digital spaces are spaces of missionary engagement like any other in today's world, warranting discerning, critical, faithful engagement. The reality is that people are increasingly inhabiting those spaces. Digital media are influential in shaping daily life. For the church to refuse to engage digitally would be to miss a significant opportunity. For digital natives growing up in digital culture, engaging these spaces is second nature. Some are more comfortable connecting with other people online than offline. They feel they can express themselves more authentically in digital spaces than physical ones. As with physical neighborhoods, there are places of abandonment, sin, division, despair, and hate online. There are also opportunities for the church to be a voice of healing, hope, reconciliation, and compassion.

In order for the church to flourish in the digital space, it will need to hold lightly some of the structural patterns that have defined the agricultural and industrial eras. Time and space work differently in the information age; people connect from many locations and at many times, rather than in one place at one time. Top-down hierarchies and command-and-control authority structures are regarded with suspicion in digital cultures shaped by networked flows of communication, sharing, and the quest for authenticity.

Ministry in digital spaces runs the risk of betraying one of the basic theological commitments of Christianity, the incarnation. Michael Frost invokes the term "excarnation" to describe a tendency in modern Western cultures to divide the spiritual from the material: "Excarnation divides life into two worlds: 1) the ideological world of idea and fantasy and story and spirituality and religious faith, and 2) the material world of action and work and building and serving and touching and caring."[11] The rise of digital culture can play into deep streams of Western culture that dualistically separate mind from body. Yet human life is lived in the flesh, and our understanding of it must be holistic. Relationships can be mediated digitally, but only at some sacrifice of their fullness.

The digital Christian community can be a very thin version of community characterized by superficial connections, little depth of accountability, "friends" who are really no more than acquaintances. and minimal actual sharing of life. Listening to a podcast of a sermon or watching a video message may be inspiring or instructive, but it doesn't take the place of walking with other disciples in community over time, sharing one another's burdens, challenging and comforting one another, and living life together. Watching a worship via livestream is qualitatively different from participating in live worship in the flesh surrounded by other bodies. Even allowing for differences in sacramental theology, breaking, eating, and sharing eucharistic bread and wine in person together is a different experience from a scattering of people in their living rooms serving themselves.

This is where digital ministry is best viewed as a complement to or pathway toward participation in local, physical ministry. Following an incarnate messiah is incarnational work that plays out in webs of relationships in local places. If the church wants to meet people where they are today, the church must be present in digital culture. But it must not lose the deeply incarnational gospel of Jesus that is experienced in communities shaped by the Spirit's power and characterized by holistic, transformed life.

CHAPTER 7

The Mixed Ecology: A Contemporary Case Study

St. Mary's Stoke was founded in 1300 in the Old Stoke area of Ipswich, a city on the Eastern coast of England. It is a medieval stone church with a young vicar, Sophie Cowan. Cowan has young children and a vision for sharing the gospel of Jesus with her diverse neighbors. The surrounding neighborhood is socioeconomically distressed, which is Cowan's own personal background.

Before Cowan arrived, the congregation had dwindled to a small number of elderly members who had mostly moved out of the immediate neighborhood long ago. Today, the Sunday morning "traditional family service" looks quite different. Alongside legacy members, worshippers from a variety of global backgrounds not only sing traditional hymns, but sing and clap along as the children and youth lead them in contemporary songs. The sermon is delivered as a thoughtful conversation without notes. The vicar's presence and style are warm and down-to-earth, and there is animated chatter before and after the service. This renewal is directly linked to some experiments that have been taking place on the edges of the church's life.

After Sunday worship, a "Top Up Shop" (food shelf) is held in the parish hall during coffee hour so parishioners can interface over tea and cake with neighbors coming for food and toiletries. Each shopper is charged a nominal fee, reflecting the premise that this is a shop where you can "top up" your pantry for the week, not just a charity. A large map of the world hangs on one of the parish hall walls where visitors and members from different countries can write their name, identify where they are from, and submit a prayer request.

Before the Top Up Shop opens, anyone interested is invited to join a 15-minute "spiritual extra" called Seeds of Hope in a separate room adjacent to the parish hall. It includes the reading of a scripture story, a short reflection, prayers, and a song. A number of men, women, and children attend, not yet ready for or interested in worship in the sanctuary across the churchyard, or perhaps working a job that makes it impossible for them to attend earlier in the morning. It's a great way to offer a simple taste of Christian worship without making people sit through an hour-long service that might well feel foreign and intimidating.

Noticing the number of parents with small children filing past her church en route to preschool and back home later in the day, Cowan thought about how busy they must be (something she experiences firsthand as a parent). She experimented with an idea called "Perfect Peace" which is part of a wider experiment called "Baby Steps." Baby Steps is a play and social time for children ages 0-5 and their caregivers offered during the week. At the end, Cowan invites parents and their children to rest on bean bag chairs for 15 minutes, turns down the lights so they can see the beautiful strings of white lights illuminating the parish hall, and plays contemplative music. After this rest time, she invites parents to share with their children what they see in them, and to have simple, uninterrupted conversation. As you can imagine, hardly anyone wants to get up off their bean bag chair when the 15 minutes are up.

St. Mary's Stoke has engaged in other experiments to try to connect with their neighbors, including a Welcome Café and a neighborhood youth group. It is an example of a mixed ecology church—an inherited church (with a long inheritance!) that is reaching out to its diverse community in simple but effective ways, forming relationships, sharing treasures from its Anglican Christian tradition, and learning how to connect with and speak to new and culturally-diverse generations.

The Emergence of the Contemporary Mixed Ecology in the UK

There are many historic church buildings like St. Mary Stoke across the UK, and most of them don't see their neighbors at Sunday worship. A 2021 census found that, for the first time, less than half (46 percent) of residents of England and Wales identified as Christian.[1] But this number is misleading, because only somewhere between 5-10 percent of the UK population actively engages in church of any kind. Many of those are global majority immigrants, especially in London and other major cities. The Church of England, which remains the state church, draws about 1 percent of the UK population on an average Sunday.[2]

This chapter explores the UK and the Church of England specifically as a case study of a mixed ecology church. The reality of deepening secularization and religious disconnection forms the backdrop for the conversation. While the UK landscape is full of the visible legacy of Christendom (in the form of cathedrals and parish church buildings, bishops sitting in the House of Lords, and the Archbishop of Canterbury presiding at royal weddings and coronations), there is no denying the deep crisis Christianity faces there. Christians in the UK are, in the words of Stuart Murray, "a vast minority."[3] "Vast" describes the significant number still identifying as Christian, but also the resources (financial, physical, cultural) that remain from the Christendom era. What is unusual is to be a minority church that was once a majority church.

The need for missionary engagement with modern Britain has long been recognized, particularly as involvement in church began to drop in the middle of the 20th century (and for men, even earlier, after World War I). A series of evangelism and church planting initiatives emerged in the 1970s and 80s, with mixed results. Church planting prior to the 1970s tended to be a daughter church model, where churches were started out of an existing parish in an area of population growth. They were geographically based and largely replicated the inherited church.[4]

What began to shift after that time was a recognition of the cultural diversity present in English communities. A 1994 report, *Breaking New Ground*, acknowledged the changes taking place in how people relate and connect in daily life: "Many in the Church of England, and not just those involved in church planting, are asking for recognition that human life is lived in a complex array of networks and that the neighborhoods, where people reside, may hold only a very minor loyalty."[5] The inherited Christendom parish system assumed people would connect to their local geographical parish church. Yet that wasn't happening as patterns of life were changing. Alongside traditional neighborhoods were networks, in which *place* was less important than *flows* of communication, relationship, and connection facilitated by technology. The rise of a "network society" has brought a growing displacement from inherited patterns of life in local communities.[6]

The doctrine of the incarnation plays a central role in Anglican theology, both historically and today: "Anglicans aim to follow the pattern of the incarnation—to be with people where they are, how they are."[7] If the inherited parish system addressed "where" they are, the emerging network culture is more about "how" they are. What was recognized even in the 1990s was that "no one strategy will be adequate to fulfill the Anglican incarnational principle in Britain today."[8] The incarnational emphasis offered a theological foundation for embodying the church in all spaces of life and community. Claiming this deep, historical theological commitment freed the Church of England to take the risks of radically reimagining what its life might look like.

As George Lings, a researcher of the mixed ecology in the UK, writes:

> Anglicanism [around 1960 and earlier] might be characterized as a Sunday gathering, conducted in a consecrated building, using the Book of Common Prayer (BCP), led by a full-time clergyman for people drawn from one parish, itself connected to a diocese and its bishop who was rather remote, appearing only at

> confirmations and institutions. These landmarks have virtually disappeared as essential components of being Anglican.[9]

Embracing incarnational contextualization (being the church with people where and how they are in today's changing cultural environment) gave license to widen what counts as "church." The Church of England drew on a deep traditional commitment (incarnational theology) as a tap root from which to draw inspiration for innovation and adaptation. In this sense, becoming a mixed ecology was a "traditional" thing for Anglicans to do. The Church of England aims to be "a Christian presence in every community."[10] Doing so requires meeting people in the complexity of where and how they are and speaking their language.

Church Planting

The first wave of mixed ecology innovation came in the form of church planting. Bob and Mary Hopkins, who had lived in Brazil and were inspired by church multiplication models in Thailand, played a key role beginning in the early 1980s when they saw themselves as cross-cultural missionaries as part of a church planting team in Lancashire. While the church growth movement had been introduced to the UK from the United States, it focused on growing the *membership* of existing churches. Church planting concentrated on growing the *number* of churches in order to reach the diversity of people in English contexts—a shift from addition to multiplication.[11] The Church of England sees church planting as a journey of contextualization:

> Church planting is the process by which a seed of the life and message of Jesus embodied by a community of Christians is immersed for mission reasons in a particular cultural or geographic context. The intended consequence is that it roots there, coming to life as a new indigenous body of Christian disciples well suited to continue in mission.[12]

This definition recognizes that the planting process will lead to adaptation as Christian life, community, and witness become indigenously present in a particular cultural context.

Holy Trinity Brompton Church (HTB) in London became a catalyst for church planting and church revitalization, particularly within the evangelical/charismatic wing of the Church of England. One model they embraced is the "resource church" model of planting and revitalization described in chapter 3, which involves sending a team of 25-40 people with a priest to an existing urban parish that had diminished to the point of irrelevance in its neighborhood. Or they might use a public space (like a nightclub or event venue) to draw people to a dynamic, culturally-accessible worship experience. Through this approach, a number of dormant Church of England parish churches were reanimated and experienced significant growth.[13] HTB also developed the Alpha course, which has had a significant impact domestically and globally as a way to introduce people to the Christian faith within the context of a shared meal and discussion.

The early decades of church planting in the late 20th century brought tensions within the inherited structure. There were controversies about new churches being planted within existing geographical parish boundaries and worries about "sheep stealing." The legacy rules weren't designed to support the kind of variation that began to emerge in what church could look like. Leaders found themselves having to carve out space for new churches while negotiating the reactions and conflicting expectations of other local clergy, bishops, and legacy church members. The theological education system at the time was largely not designed to train leaders for this kind of work. Yet there was a growing wave of experimentation in cultivating new Christian communities.

Alternative Worship Communities

Forms of church contextualized for specific populations that didn't neatly fit into the "church planting" box began to emerge more significantly in the later 1980s and into the early 2000s. One of these is alternative worship communities, which began to be referred to as "alt.worship." These communities sought to recontextualize worship for a postmodern age. Visions, which began in York in 1991, combined traditional elements of worship (Eucharist, robes, processions, candles, incense, sacred chants) with creative ways of engaging young adults such as trip-hop beats, projected images, video loops, and prayer stations. This all took place within the very traditional space of York Minster, one of England's major cathedrals.[14] Grace is another community that emerged in the early 1990s and continues to this day in the Ealing area of West London. They developed creative monthly worship services featuring interactive stations, video, discussions, ambient music, and a cafe with food and wine.[15]

Alternative worship communities, some of which have survived and others of which have concluded their life cycles, can be seen as attempts to recontextualize worship within a participatory, postmodern culture. They tend to stress creativity, the arts, personal engagement, and conversation rather than performance by a preacher, choir, or worship band that is passively consumed by the people. One of the difficulties for their sustainability is the investment of time and energy required to develop each service. They also focus on worship, where traditional church growth and church planting also tend to focus. Worship is a key point of contact for people with church backgrounds. Many people with no experience of church would likely find these alt.worship communities more culturally accessible than traditional forms of worship were they to show up. But most people with no experience of church aren't showing up at worship services. They have to be reached in other ways.

Fresh Expressions of Church

In 2011 a peaceful protest in the Tottenham area of North London following the shooting death of Mark Duggan, a local Black man, by a police officer devolved into rioting and looting, which spread to towns and cities across England, fueled by social media. Launched in 2013 as a way to foster community and healing, the Engine Room is a community center with a cafe, nursery, and three meeting rooms regularly hosting birthday parties, anniversaries, wedding celebrations, trainings, and business meetings. On Saturdays the Muslim community gathers for prayer in one of the larger spaces, and during the week there are activities for every age group, running the gamut from art workshops, homework clubs, a youth program, yoga, and street dance, to a Pioneer Girlz group for 11- to 18-year olds. On Thursdays a Pop Up Cafe for children and parents takes place outside the local primary school.

In 2013 a small Christian community serving the people of Hale Village, Ferry Lane, and Bream Close estates began worshiping in a temporary space. When a worship space located in the Engine Room in Hale Village was completed in October 2017, this group moved in and St. Francis at the Engine Room was born. The church meets each Sunday for an informal Eucharist. On the last Sunday of each month, a "bring and share" lunch following the service enables the worshiping community to get to know each other better. The chapel is always open for prayer and reflection. Father Andrew Williams, one of two priests serving the Tottenham Hale community, is grateful that St. Francis' location enables members of this community to live their Christian faith by "sharing what they have, caring for their local community, and working with anyone who wants to improve people's lives."[16]

This story is an example of a fresh expression of church.[17] As explored in chapter 4, fresh expressions are "new forms of church that emerge within contemporary culture and engage primarily with people who don't 'go to church.'"[18] The phrase "fresh expressions of church" comes from the ordination service for Church of England clergy, which states, "The Church of England . . . professes the faith uniquely revealed in the Holy Scriptures and set forth in the catholic creeds, which faith the Church is called to proclaim afresh in each generation."[19] Michael Moynagh describes them as "church in life"—Christian communities that emerge within the ordinary spaces of neighborhood life through a process of relationships, listening, and loving first, rather than making worship the initial point of contact.[20]

A seminal report issued in 2004 by the Archbishop's Council on Mission and Public Affairs of the Church of England, titled *Mission-Shaped Church*, provided an analysis of the missionary situation of Christianity in the UK and described and endorsed a range of what it called "fresh expressions of church." These included alternative worship communities, Base Ecclesial Communities, cell churches, cafe churches, network-focused churches, new monastic communities, school-based churches, and youth congregations.[21] *Mission-Shaped Church* embraced the premise that a wide diversity of forms of Christian community were necessary to live into the Church of England's incarnational mission.

Since the early 2000s, fresh expressions have become widespread across the UK. A major 2016 study found over 1,100 fresh expressions within a sample of 21 dioceses (half of the total in the Church of England). At the time these made up 15 percent of the church communities in these dioceses, with over 50,000 people attending, or about 10 percent of the overall attendance. The average size was about 50 active participants.

The vast majority are started by a local parish church and remain closely connected to it. Fresh expressions participants are made up of 4 percent Christians, 27 percent dechurched, and 33 percent non-churched. More than a third are led by lay leaders with no formal theological training. They are about as likely to be led by women as men.[22]

The category of fresh expressions has provided a framework in which to explore and experiment with a diversity of contextualized Christian communities on the edges of the church's life. Many of these are experimental and provisionary, lasting for a season rather than developing a long-term lifespan. They have become vehicles for meaningful Christian witness in a post-Christian society while also allowing the church to learn how to be in mission with people in today's culture who are disconnected from religious faith. Fresh expressions have also been ways to reactivate Christian practice and participation among those who have fallen away and for whom traditional church is inaccessible or inhospitable.

A Theological Vision for the Mixed Ecology

In his foreword to the seminal *Mission-Shaped Church* report, Rowan Williams, who served as archbishop of Canterbury from 2002-2012, wrote:

> If 'church' is what happens when people encounter the Risen Jesus and commit themselves to sustaining and deepening that encounter in their encounter with each

> other, there is plenty of theological room for diversity of rhythm and style, so long as we have ways of identifying the same living Christ at the heart of every expression of Christian life in common.[23]

Part of the Church of England's journey over the past two decades has been to wrestle theologically with how fresh expressions, church plants, and other emerging forms of contextual Christian community fit within its theological and ecclesiological framework. Anglicanism sees itself as part of the universal (catholic) church, anchored by scripture, the creeds, the sacraments of baptism and Eucharist, and the historic episcopate. What does it mean theologically to embrace the mixed ecology?

Mission-Shaped Church offered an initial theological rationale, beginning with what has become a central understanding within ecumenical mission theology: the triune God is a missionary God (*missio Dei*). God's trinitarian life is a communion of persons whose love overflows to create the world and restore it to right relationships when it becomes estranged. God is active in the local context and mission involves discernment and participation in God's work in the world. Christ becomes incarnate to take on a specific cultural identity in solidarity and love, leading to ongoing translation of the gospel into every culture. The incarnation leads to the cross, Christ's costly countercultural stance and self-sacrifice within his own cultural situation. Jesus's ministry is about the kingdom of God, which is about breaking down social boundaries, hope for the poor, and God's welcome of all. The church bears witness to the kingdom in the power of the Spirit.[24]

Mission-Shaped Church stressed four relationships that define the church as "one, holy, catholic, and apostolic" (from the Nicene Creed). The first of these is the *up* dimension, the relationship with God through worship and becoming holy (sanctification). The second is the *in* dimension, which is about relationships of unity in diversity, reflecting the life of the Trinity and the richness of God's creation. The third is the church's sentness, its journey *out* in apostolic witness. Finally, every expression of church is part *of* the wider universal church.[25]

Michael Moynagh uses the biblical metaphor of "tents, synagogues, and temples" as a way to reimagine the mixed ecology of church. "Temples" are where people connect with the larger body of Christ—conferences, retreats, celebrations, pilgrimages, and websites. Just as Jesus went to the Jerusalem Temple periodically, so too do believers engage these communal offerings and gatherings at times. "Synagogues" are conventional local churches as a primary focus of spiritual connection and engagement. "Tents" are small worshiping communities within the spaces of daily life. Just as the people of Israel inhabited tents on the journey through the wilderness, tents in today's church may be fruitful for a period but also more flexible and adaptable than synagogues and temples.[26] Some people who have been part of tents may gravitate toward synagogues, desiring a more regular or traditional rhythm of worship. Synagogue participants may find tents more participatory, and their gatherings in workplaces or the outdoors more accessible and expansive. Many people may find that different ways of gathering in different contexts feeds their souls and provides them more ways to grow in their relationship with God and others.

The introduction of the mixed ecology within the life of the Church of England has not been without theological controversy. Writers such as Andrew Davison, Alison Milbank, and Martyn Percy have criticized fresh expressions for abandoning the historic parish ideal and the richness of its traditions. They fear fresh expressions and contextualized forms of church focused on one cultural or social group will betray the diversity of what it means to be a local body of Christ.[27] The challenge for those who exclusively embrace a traditional parish model of church is that this model remains disconnected from the overwhelming majority of its neighbors. The power of a mixed ecology approach is that it makes space for a variety of models alongside one another.

Strategy and Structure

The cultivation of a mixed ecology of church over the past few decades in the Church of England did not happen by accident. While the initial green shoots emerged as local, organic, Spirit-led initiatives, the denomination as a system eventually organized formal support. Without this intentionality, it is unlikely that so much innovation and creativity would have occurred. While the evolution of the mixed ecology in the Church of England (and the UK more broadly) is still a work in progress, there are several key elements worth noting.

The Role of Networks

Informal networks emerged around church planting in the 1980s and around alt.worship and fresh expressions in the 90s and 2000s.

Later, the Fresh Expressions organization within the Church of England connected and equipped local practitioners. Vision, stories, and practices have been shared across these networks, including through a DVD series, information sessions, trainings, and a website. For those starting something new, being connected to other practitioners and thought leaders is essential. From early on in the UK, these networks were ecumenical, initially with the British Methodists, then also with the Reformed Church.

Leadership from the Top

The mixed ecology was affirmed and authorized by the highest institutional levels of the Church of England. The publication of key reports from national church councils, especially the *Mission-Shaped Church* report, affirmed what was taking place and expanded the imagination of the whole denomination around what was possible. The role of Rowan Williams, who as a diocesan bishop intentionally sought out and supported experiments on the edges of the church's life, is particularly vital to note. When he became archbishop of Canterbury (the Church of England's senior bishop), he cast vision for the mixed ecology and offered theological support. Other bishops, such as Graham Cray, Steven Croft, and Mike Harrison, provided leadership and permission from within the hierarchy.

Structure and Resourcing

Early on, a group of senior business leaders who recognized both the church's crisis and the opportunity to do something about it came together as the "Lambeth Partners" to invest in resourcing innovation. They provided resources, strategic counsel, and accountability to the teams leading the work. The development of structures within the churchwide organization of the Church of England brought this work into the heart of the institution. In later years, this devolved to the dioceses once it had taken root. Resources from the Church of England's endowments are being distributed to dioceses for investments in mixed ecology innovation. Permission was also created within the canonical (legal) structures for alternative forms of church through "Bishop's Mission Orders," which legitimized and licensed new Christian communities within existing parish boundaries. This provided accountability and support within the larger system.[28]

Leader Training

The mixed ecology needs a different kind of leader and leadership education than traditional churches. Within the Church of England, this has taken place in a range of forms. "Pioneer" training courses were developed within existing theological colleges and institutions.[29] Training organizations for church planting like the Gregory Centre for Church Multiplication have emerged.[30] Since many fresh expressions are lay-led, informal training was developed through initiatives that provide just-in-time resources for leaders in local small groups. The Church of England developed a set of criteria for ordained pioneer ministers.[31] One-on-one mentorship of a lay or ordained pioneer by a priest was another way to apprentice and support those called to lead a fresh expression and provide needed accountability.[32]

There are now multiple pathways within a variety of institutions for leaders to be equipped for this journey.

Conclusion

The Church of England's vision for the 2020s is to be a Jesus-centered church for the whole nation that is *simpler*, *humbler*, and *bolder*.[33] This vision acknowledges the post-Christendom reality of learning how to offer embodied witness to the gospel on simpler and humbler terms than Christendom assumed. The boldness and clear commitment to being Jesus-centered speaks to the need to clarify and renew the church's identity in Christ. This vision is accompanied by three priorities:

- **To become a church of missionary disciples**—where all God's people are free to live the Christian life, wherever we spend our time Sunday to Saturday.
- **To be a church where mixed ecology is the norm**—where every person in England has access to an enriching and compelling community of faith by adding new churches and new forms of church to our parishes, cathedrals, schools, and chaplaincies.
- **To be a church that is younger and more diverse.**[34]

Becoming a church of missionary disciples rather than nominal cultural or institutional Christians involves reinvigorating spiritual practices and faith in daily life. Making the mixed ecology the norm gives space and permission for the complexity of different forms of Christian community required to be church for the whole nation. Becoming a church that is younger and more diverse necessitates experimenting with contextualized witness, worship, and Christian community life.

For readers in the United States or other global contexts, we offer this case study to shed light on how a very old church system burdened by centuries of establishment and history can make space for creative new forms of Christian life and witness. Needless to say, there are key differences in the United States context relative to the UK. While formal disestablishment of the church in America happened long ago, cultural establishment remains more vigorous, particularly in regions such as the South. American Christianity has an organizational dynamism and optimism that is less the case in Europe. Yet trends toward religious disaffiliation in America are headed in the European direction, especially generationally. Nearly a third of American adults identify as "nothing in particular" on religious identity surveys, almost 70 percent of whom are under age 50.[35]

Church growth and Christian engagement in Britain in the past decades have been driven in significant part by Black, Asian, and minority ethnic communities, many of whom are recent immigrants.[36] The Church of England has at times struggled to receive and embrace the gifts of these Christian migrants. Many Anglican migrants from global majority contexts don't find in white British congregations the dynamic, expressive, and charismatic expressions of worship, faith, and theology they are used to, and some end up in African- or Asian-led Pentecostal churches instead. A mixed ecology must include a wide range of cultural expressions of church life and worship. The presence of global majority Christians within white-majority cultures such as the United States and UK offers an opportunity to receive the gospel afresh from siblings in Christ in cultural forms that are not domesticated by Western modernity.[37]

In all this, it is critical to recognize that the 20th century secularization thesis for Western societies has been proven wrong. It is not true that cultures become inexorably more secular under the influence of modernity; the reality is much more complex. Michael Moynagh observes that in the UK, *Mission-Shaped Church* offered a hypothesis that social change does not make church demise inevitable. Rather, the problem has been the church's failure to adapt. New contextual churches are the Spirit's means of reversing decline.[38]

The Church of England can best be described as "on the way" toward transformation. Much more work is yet to be done. There remains a good deal of fragility in the system, particularly as the Church of England negotiates issues of sexuality at the time of this writing that may lead to division. However, the need for an expanded framework for how Christian community can and should be embodied to reach a changing culture has been established. There is active work underway to start thousands of new Christian communities that will reach people who don't currently identify as Christian or participate in church. Theological understandings and practical pathways have been developed to undergird and support the work. For denominations and church systems in other contexts, a key lesson is to start this journey early. The Church of England began relatively late, when the process of decline was already deeply underway. This created a sense of urgency, but it also means that many places in the system are so weak they have little capacity to try new things.[39]

CHAPTER 8

Making Space, Learning, and Leading Together

Lightwave is a networked community of experimental expressions of church within the largely rural Diocese of St. Edmundsbury and Ipswich in the Church of England. As the diocese began to cultivate and encourage fresh expressions of church over the past few decades, leaders realized that it was vital to create a structure that would enable a greater variety to flourish, especially in rural areas. The Lightwave Community is a "Bishop's Mission Order," a category of ecclesial entity within the Church of England created to recognize alternative forms of church focused on reaching people who don't normally go to church. It has its own status as a registered charity (nonprofit organization) and a board of trustees, but exists within the larger structure of the diocese with the full support of the diocesan leadership.[1]

As of this writing, Lightwave encompasses over 20 fresh expressions of church scattered across the Suffolk region of East England. It values high levels of participation, becoming disciples, creating community, evangelism, and encountering God. As they focus on sharing faith, Lightwave groups have become involved in combating isolation and poverty, engaging youth, caring for creation, and agricultural chaplaincy. The Lightwave Community is led by Sally Gaze, archdeacon for rural mission in the diocese, and she oversees the various groups. A small central team equips, connects, and supports Lightwave group leaders and holds them accountable. The work of starting new forms of church can be lonely and thankless. Lightwave provides a network of prayer, mutual encouragement, and inspiration.

A Lightwave group's approach is first to listen prayerfully to God and discern what God is doing in a local context. Grassroots leaders seek to offer practical love to neighbors in ways that create community. Out of this, new forms of church arise. Lightwave draws on outside training resources such as Myriad (a lay-led church planting network in the UK[2]) and Greenhouse (a training resource for fresh expressions pioneers). At the regional level, it provides an incubator for new forms of Christian community to emerge and grow without having to go it alone. Lightwave is an ecclesial framework that allows things to happen that otherwise wouldn't in an inherited system designed largely for different purposes. The commitments that shape Lightwave's work are also now becoming embedded in the inherited diocesan structure. For instance, priests coming into the diocese to take a call have to commit in their contracts to enabling two new worshiping communities to emerge in their local contexts within five years.

Living into a Both/And Way of Being Church

Organizational and leadership scholar John Kotter observes that the pace of change in today's world is such that the basic systems, structures, and cultures built up over the past centuries can't keep pace with the demands being placed on them:

> Incremental adjustments to how you manage and strategize, no matter how clever, are not up to the job. You need something new to stay ahead in an age of tumultuous change and growing uncertainties. The solution is not to trash what we know and start over but instead to reintroduce, in an organic way, a second system—one which would be familiar to most successful entrepreneurs. The new system adds needed agility and speed while the old one, which keeps running, provides reliability and efficiency.[3]

Kotter proposes a *dual operating system*—retaining the inherited structure for sustaining the traditional parts of the organization that are still functioning, but adding a new structure that is more like a startup within the midst of the old. The new system brings values and freedom that the old system is not designed for, such as permission to take risks and fail, flexibility of rules and procedures, rapid cycles of iterative learning, and authorization and empowerment of leaders who might not fit into the traditional boxes. Since inherited organizations tend to be focused on sustaining the status quo, they will always struggle to make space for the kind of experimentation that is required to address the massive changes taking place in today's environment. Abandoning those established structures wholesale isn't a desirable or viable option, since they provide necessary support, accountability, and continuity for the operations of the existing organization. The resources of the inherited organization also provide vital seed funding for the emerging future.

An example of a dual operating system approach to church would be the Lightwave community existing within a centuries-old inherited system of a diocese. Lightwave is still relatively new and small, but through its experiments, the Church of England is learning how to form Christian community with neighbors in the Suffolk region in complementary ways that the inherited parish structure largely would not achieve on its own. The two systems work together collaboratively. Lightwave is able to bring opportunities through an agile system parallel to and working closely with the traditional structures.

A mixed ecology approach to church says that we need the inherited forms and emerging forms to thrive alongside one another in mutuality. Together, they make possible what would otherwise not happen. The mixed ecology affirms and values traditional forms of church while also recognizing that they are no longer sufficient to reach most of today's neighbors in a changing culture. The legacy members of traditional churches should not be abandoned. Yet if everything in the church's life is normed around the expressions of church that work for them and not their neighbors, the church will have no future and fail at its basic mission of making disciples of all nations.

In the Diocese of St. Edmundsbury and Ipswich, the vast majority of fresh expressions emerge, wholly or partly, from within the life of an inherited parish church. Three-fourths of the leaders of these new forms of church have a direct, life-giving mutual relationship with the inherited parish church in their context. Some of the new Christians who discover the power of the gospel through these emerging communities end up joining traditional churches. Legacy members of inherited churches are involved in launching and supporting alternative new communities. It is a wonderfully fluid and messy dynamic, all within the larger structure of one church body.

In chapter 6, we talked about some of the differences between traditional communities, bureaucracies, and networks. Our inherited church systems were largely organized for either a traditional community or bureaucratic paradigm. For instance, the parish system of neighborhood churches assumes people will participate in their local neighborhood or village church by nature of geographical proximity. Many of these churches were started before the automobile brought greater mobility and choice of which congregation to join. In the 20th century, bureaucracies sought to bring efficiency, uniformity, and standardization across the church. Many denominational structures that had functioned more informally and relationally adopted rigid policies, procedures, and standardized norms—for instance in the credentialing of leaders and the categorization of different forms of church.

Today, digital technology, mobility, and changing patterns of relationship and association are leading to the breakdown of both traditional communities and bureaucracies. The bureaucratic impulse toward control and conformity is not serving the church well in a time in which we need greater diversity of expression, permission to experiment, and new learning. Bureaucracies are designed around the assumption that experts at the center or the top have the answers that should be implemented at the grassroots level. That is often not the case in the face of today's challenges. The learning needs to emerge on the edges and at the local level through cycles of experimentation. To the extent to which bureaucratic denominational and regional church structures insist on uniformity and centralized control, the more difficult the necessary work of adaptation and recontextualization will be.

We now live in an increasingly networked society. Networks bring significant gifts to this moment when the challenges the church is facing have no easy answers. Rather than create new bureaucracies within the inherited ones, leaders might cultivate networks dedicated to learning, connection, mutual support, and collaboration. Many bureaucratic systems are collapsing of their own weight, and expending energy trying to fix and tweak them within their existing organizational paradigm will not yield much fruit. What will replace today's inherited denominational and regional church structures will probably look much more like networks than bureaucracies.

At the same time, it isn't fully clear yet what kinds of local and regional organizational structures will be needed to support the emerging future. New structures must have the authority and freedom to organize themselves for different purposes than ensuring uniformity and command-and-control. They can connect local leaders and communities that are experimenting on the edges of the church's life. The culture of emerging structures should embrace clarity about the values guiding the work, a high tolerance of failure, habits of action-reflection that allow participants to learn from their experiments, and, above all, a spirit of discernment as they seek God's leading.

The mixed ecology is a way to think about fostering new ways of relating and organizing within inherited systems. Sally Gaze uses the metaphor of a garden, where some churches might be like a great old oak tree, taking a lot of space and established over many years, while other churches are more like strawberry plants that multiply quickly to cover the ground but may be more transitory and fragile in their individual form. The garden is the richer for the presence of both.[4]

One of the fears leaders often have of embracing networked structures rather than bureaucratic hierarchies is the loss of identity. If identity can't be enforced through regulation and uniformity, isn't it in danger of being eroded? This is where interpretive leadership is essential. Leaders are responsible for helping the community identify and own the guiding values that shape the church's life and mission. Such clear values—the core story we are formed around—become the touchstone to refer back to. One of the greatest gifts leaders can give church communities or systems right now is to guide processes of interpretation and articulation of theological identity. This is all the more urgent in a post-Christian society where the church can no longer assume people know the church's story. Many neighbors *think* they know the church's story and have rejected it, but their assumptions about what Christians actually believe may be far from the truth.

Learning on the Edges

The Jesus movement began on the edges of two established systems—first century Palestinian Judaism and the Roman

Empire. Jesus led his followers (apprentices) in practices of healing, compassion, and transformation that gave witness to an alternative ordering of reality—the reign or kingdom of God. This movement began from below, with ordinary people like fishermen and tradespeople and outsiders like tax collectors and prostitutes. As we consider the mixed ecology today, this location is vital to recall. God's future is often already present but unrecognized because it lives among the people the dominant systems ignore or neglect.

Living into the mixed ecology today means paying attention to the edges of the church's life. We need to ask the question of what God might be up to in the lives of our neighbors and local communities and identify God's invitations to join God's movement there. This calls for practices of presence, relationship, compassionate listening, discernment, and participation. On the contrary, many inherited church structures are designed more for performance and programs. This is why it is essential to cultivate alternative spaces within and around inherited church structures to do this work of learning without the expectation that it will result immediately in material benefits to the existing institution. Inherited churches can sometimes function as complex programmatic systems that feed on a lot of energy and resources. It can be difficult to make space within their life for this kind of simple, humble listening and experimentation in neighborhood spaces.

Leaders of all sorts called to thrive on the edges of the church's life should be given permission and encouragement to incarnate Christian life there rather than being pulled into managing the inherited church machine and its expectations.

This is where the paradigm shift from primarily clergy-led, lay-supported ministry to primarily lay-led, clergy-supported ministry is helpful. Clergy can refocus their work primarily as spiritual and theological interpreters rooted in the traditions of Christian faith who equip God's people to join God's mission of love, healing, and community creation and restoration. This means multiplying leadership according to gifts and calling and expanding our categories of who qualifies as a leader. Already in many church systems there is a lack of clergy to fill positions in the inherited church. This work of learning on the edges cannot be one more thing added to a long list of expectations of clergy responsible for managing the existing system. God has leaders in the church who are called to this work, but inherited systems often don't recognize and authorize them.

Churches today need a more generous understanding of church leadership that moves beyond the clerical and professional models to embrace a wide range of types of leaders in different roles working together. This might mean lay leaders being encouraged to invest presence and relationship in the local communities where they already have connections as God's ambassadors and starters of new ministries. It might mean multi-vocational callings. It might mean lay leaders stepping into greater authority and responsibility in managing inherited church structures so that clergy can dedicate more time to spiritual and theological leadership and less time on administration. It will certainly mean a more collaborative model in which a variety of gifts are activated and work together for the sake of the flourishing of the whole. Ministry in teams will require normative rather than solo leadership.

The cultural and ecclesial assumptions shaping how leaders are identified, trained, credentialed, and deployed warrant scrutiny in a time when the context is rapidly changing. The Holy Spirit is raising up leaders across the churches today with a passion for the gospel and fresh imagination for how to do church with people outside established congregational structures. Many of those leaders are people of color. Yet the inherited structures often struggle to recognize their gifts and callings, place overly heavy burdens and restrictions on their formation and credentialing, or withhold the resources required for their ministries to flourish in sustainable ways. These emerging leaders are sometimes expected to fit into boxes designed for a different era and different kind of leader and Christian community. Such leaders can find themselves discouraged, excluded, and rejected by the very church systems who need their gifts to discover a faithful and hopeful future.

Integration in Practice

On its website, St. Peter's, Bethnal Green describes itself as "an eclectic church community in the heart of East London, here to worship God, make friends, and change the world." St. Peter's revitalization began when a team from Holy Trinity Brompton (HTB) arrived alongside the dwindling legacy St. Peter's congregation. Initially, the HTB team didn't change anything. They focused on listening to and building relationships with the small group of longtime members over tea. During these conversations the newcomers learned that St. Peter's vacuum cleaner was broken. The team went out and bought the congregation a vacuum. Over time the incoming team built enough trust to introduce a guitar, a box drum, and a more conversational tone in the later worship service.

St. Peter's first service is a more traditional Anglican Book of Common Prayer service conducted in a relaxed spirit. It is small. The second service is different. Lay preachers are not uncommon, and the pews are full of young adults. After the sermon worshippers are asked to stand up and share how the Holy Spirit has been working in their lives during the past week. The majority of church members stand up and share about recent health scares, persecution at work for being a Christian, and exciting developments in the church's coaching program for unemployed young adults. Both services share a coffee hour in the back of the church by the entrance, including tea and refreshments. When the music volume increases, second service participants begin to make their way toward the pews. A few older members attend both services.

St. Peter's building was built in the 1840s. Small white lights strung throughout the church make it feel warm and cheery, and sofas line the front area of the sanctuary. On Wednesdays Art & Soul, an intergenerational community arts group, is offered. Anyone interested can show up, and there is an optional opportunity to pray at the end. The church also has Life Groups that meet during the week, Alpha, and intentional groups and activities for children and youth. On Wednesdays St. Peter's offers a Zoom Morning Prayer service and a time of group prayer in the evening called "Dwell." The church also sponsors a podcast, "The Prayer Garden," to help listeners join with God and pray for the world.[5] St. Peter's, Bethnal Green has become a mixed ecology church reaching different populations through close relationships, connections, and collaboration between the legacy membership and the new leaders and participants who have come more recently.

Ed Olsworth-Peter describes four "footprints" for what an integrated mixed ecology looks like in practice.[6] The first is a *parallel* approach, where two expressions of church coexist with an exchange or movement between them. They may worship in the same building or area and some people may attend both, opting in and out, but their lives are otherwise distinct even as they prayerfully and practically support each other. They see themselves primarily as reaching two different communities in their context.

Another approach is *progression*, where two forms of church happen at different times and places, but one leads into another. For instance, an initial fresh expression with young families organized around a school might lead to a Messy Church. Or a Messy Church might lead to a weekly deeper congregational ministry with young families. One can lead as a natural stepping stone to another, and leaders in the two communities talk openly about that. There is intentionality about how different expressions of church can provide pathways for deepened belonging and commitment.

An additional approach is *partnership*, where different expressions of church are supported by a variety of resource partners. For instance, an ecumenical Messy Church may be in relationship with other local congregations in a neighborhood or village. The inherited churches may contribute volunteer leadership to the Messy Church. Or perhaps a pastor or priest from an inherited church might lead sacramental aspects of worship for a fresh expression of church.

Finally, different forms of church can serve as a *precursor*. Collaboration between different expressions of a church in a context can pave the way for a new form of church to emerge that may be different from those existing expressions. God may want to launch something new through the partnering of local forms of church. This new form in turn becomes part of the mixed ecology.

The mixed ecology invites us to assume a posture of abundance rather than scarcity or competition in ministry. In the UK and other Western societies that are more secularized than America, simply being actively Christian is a countercultural practice. Churches in the United States need to get beyond the Christendom assumption that they are primarily competing for members with each other and recognize that they are on the same team. The real competition is a pagan society and all of its false promises. When we adopt an abundance mindset we realize that God is at work through many different traditions and local expressions of church, reaching different people and responding to contextual realities. How might these various forms of church be understood together to be part of God's mission in this place? How might they then recognize the blessings and gifts each brings?

The mixed ecology is an ecumenical reality, not just within particular church bodies, systems, denominations, or traditions. Already there are countless ways in which churches partner and collaborate across denominations and traditions, whether in social ministry, pulpit-sharing, evangelism, or age-specific ministries. A mixed ecology imagination helps us see how God can be at work within many different Christian communities in a given place, with each tradition bringing its gifts. Ecumenical collaboration can be complicated politically and theologically, but it is a vital aspect of a mixed ecology church. In many places, starting a new Christian community or experimenting with contextualized forms of ministry may seem more plausible if we can identify a team of people in a local area who share a passion for the work, even if they come from multiple established churches. Given the shrinking size of many American congregations (and the rise of others that are huge but downplay denominational differences and identifications), God may already be breaking down some of these walls.

Getting Started on Embracing the Mixed Ecology

Where does the mixed ecology journey begin? We explore in the following paragraphs how leaders in a variety of locations within the church can engage the mixed ecology. But we must begin with some key shared commitments. The first is a recognition that God is at work in the world bringing forth new life even amidst change and loss. The leadership (influence) of the Holy Spirit must be primary in our lives and churches, which means we must embrace a *posture of prayerful discernment*. We must "test the spirits" (1 John 4:1) to see what is of God and what is not. The ancient practice of discernment is how Christians throughout history have sought God's leading amidst ambiguity and challenge. It is vital today. Churches in every context and at every level must learn how to identify and follow the Spirit's movement and invitation. If we try to do this on our own without the Spirit's leadership, we will go astray.

Second is a *heart of compassion for neighbors* who don't know the hope, healing, and power of abundant life in Christ. God so loved the world that he gave his only son, Jesus, so that everyone who believes in him may have eternal life (John 3:16). That expansive love includes all kinds of people far from church as we typically know it. God's heart breaks for people everywhere living in isolation, despair, addiction, injustice, estrangement, and destructive relationships with themselves, others, and the Earth. Mission is about joining God's heart of love and compassion because we know that love and compassion ourselves.

This means that the center of every community in the mixed ecology must be *the gospel of Jesus and his invitation to follow him*. If we aren't helping people live as apprentices of Jesus in the whole of life in community with one another, we're missing the central point of church. It is hard to follow Jesus in a culture that is dominated by alternative stories, forces, and practices that form us in other directions than God's reign. We must continually reflect critically together on the culture(s) we find ourselves in and discern what is of God and what is not. Discipleship (learning to live a Jesus-shaped life) must be the central focus.

At the same time, God is active in human culture and in the world creating new forms of life and community, translating and adapting the shape of the church to embody Jesus in various times and places. The creative side of the mixed ecology recognizes that creation is ongoing and God is always doing new things for us to join. *Recontextualization of the church's life* is the work of every generation. The mixed ecology assumes this is the case and provides permission and encouragement for it while affirming the treasures of time-honored ways of being church.

For *everyday disciples or lay leaders* within local churches who are curious about or eager to explore what the mixed ecology might look like in their context, a good place to begin is by noticing.[7] What forms of Christian community currently exist in your local setting? How are they related, if at all? Who are the people in your life who don't have anything to do with church but might find life with Jesus a solution to their struggles and yearnings? One practice a congregation can do is called a "Who's Missing?" exercise, where participants are invited to identify people they know who don't go to church, reflect on why they don't, and then consider what church might need to look like in order for it to be accessible and meaningful for them. Another fruitful practice is to invite people to identify where in daily life they have tastes or glimpses of "church"—where do they experience God healing others, creating community, and bringing peace outside the walls of worship and church activities? This can open up imagination for how the church might intentionally cultivate those experiences and encounters outside church walls.

Everyday disciples and lay leaders may sense God calling them to be part of a new form of Christian community. Perhaps they are called to start one or to support or participate in one on some level. The best approach is to gather another person or two to join in prayer and discernment and to pay attention together to the spaces of daily life where you are currently engaged and might be called to invest presence, relationship, and community. When Jesus sends his followers out, he sends them in pairs, not alone (Luke 10:1-12). Prayerfully seek God's invitation to listen, love, form deeper relationships, and explore spiritual questions with neighbors. This might mean remaining active in a traditional congregation while experimenting on the side with a new form of Christian community with a friend or two. Or you might be called to be part of a team that dedicates itself more fully to starting a new church or ministry. You may be engaged in multiple expressions of church and can help make connections between them.

For *local pastors and priests* serving inherited churches, embracing the mixed ecology involves recognizing the particular gifts and calling of the community entrusted to your care while acknowledging its own contextual particularity. This means that there are likely many neighbors in your context who won't find your church's worship service or Christian formation activities accessible or attractive. You can help members of your community reflect on how other forms of church might be necessary alongside what you do together every Sunday to share the gospel of Jesus with neighbors. You can begin to cultivate a mixed ecology imagination in the people of your church, inviting them to explore how they might be called to experiment with new forms of church at the edges of the congregation's life.

What this will look like will vary depending on the context and size of the congregation. At the minimum it will mean being a permission-giver, encouraging, equipping, and coaching those who might be called to start new forms of Christian community. That doesn't mean you need to start something new yourself—though you may be called to that work. It doesn't mean you need to be an expert in church planting, fresh expressions, or digital church. There are multiple training and coaching resources available.[8]

It does mean helping to articulate the *why* for this work. In many legacy congregations, the meaning and value of church are assumed rather than given careful attention and exposition. Yet people may have a range of reasons why they participate—it could be primarily for social or cultural reasons, as a vehicle for doing community service, or out of habit. In an increasingly post-Christian society, the church must be clear about its "why"—why it exists, what story animates it, and what difference it makes in people's lives. This is theological and spiritual work that must be done contextually so it makes sense to people where they are.

One of the barriers we've seen over the years to people taking the journey of helping start a new form of Christian community designed to reach neighbors who aren't part of church is a lack of motivation. Late-modern Western culture assumes every individual's path to meaning and purpose is equally valid (as long as they don't impose their private beliefs on anyone else or make them public). It rejects any ultimate public framework for truth other than its own secular, relativist one. Many faithful members of local churches have been shaped by this cultural ideology without even recognizing how deeply it contradicts the gospel of Jesus. There is no "neutral" place to stand by which to evaluate worldviews and faith claims. Every position has deep assumptions embedded in it, and the late modern secular one is no different.

The journey of exploring the mixed ecology can be an invitation for local churches to think theologically about their life and context and ask hard questions about gospel and culture. What story do we have to offer as the church? How are we embodying it in our life and practices? How might we interpret or translate it so that our neighbors can understand and receive it? This work of tending and clarifying theological identity and spiritual practices is essential for this season of the church's life. New ministries that aren't clear about what is at their core and what values animate them won't likely succeed. Established ministries have the benefit of legacy members, resources, and momentum, but as cultural winds shift away from church participation, they also will need to get clearer about who they are and what they offer to the world that is different from other organizations.

For *leaders of regional church systems and denominations*, the mixed ecology is a blueprint for how to imagine, recognize, and support a rich diversity of forms of Christian church and mission together. This begins by recognizing the changed cultural environment and the need for experimentation and new learning in mission. It also requires accepting that inherited bureaucratic forms of church organization that enforce uniformity and standardization no longer serve us well. There are several key steps that leaders of church systems can make.

The first is to help the church interpret this moment through truth-telling about the disintegration of many inherited church structures and the cultural reasons underneath it. Candor and realism about the institutional challenges need not lead to despair. Our hope is in God, not human institutions, and the church has been through cycles of growth, decline, and adaptation throughout its history. This is not the end of the church, even as it may be the end of certain institutional forms of church. Refocusing people in the system on the core work of cultivating disciples of Jesus in contemporary culture provides new energy and hopefulness. This begins with grounding everything we do in the biblical narrative and introducing simple spiritual practices that help people connect more deeply with God, each other, and their neighbors.

The second step is to begin to cultivate a dual operating system by identifying, forming, and encouraging networks of grassroots leaders called to innovate alternative expressions of church. This might mean dedicating some staff time and resources to this work rather than being consumed entirely by managing the inherited operation. It requires giving permission for new forms of church to emerge, even if they don't fit into the old boxes. This might involve suspending some rules and regulations to make space for experiments and learning until it is clear what new policies are adequate to ensure good governance. Examples like Bishop's Mission Orders in the Church of England are fruitful in this regard, as they create organizational space within the system for things the inherited church can't imagine.

Alternative pathways for leader training and credentialing are essential in systems designed more or less exclusively for 20th century professional clergy. Many churches have in their own history far more flexible and local approaches to educating leaders that can be reclaimed for a new era. For instance, before the seminary system emerged in the early 1800s, many clergy "read for orders" under the mentorship and guidance of a local pastor or priest. This is already taking place again today. Online platforms like Luther Seminary's Faith+Lead can resource this education with affordable, accessible on-demand digital courses.[9]

Regional church systems and denominations can function as networks of learning, collaboration, and sharing as they adapt their life from focusing on maintenance, management, and governance to learning, equipping, and discovery. Regional church systems in particular can cultivate a high-challenge, high-support environment in which the realities of a changing world create a strong sense of urgency but there are clear pathways for new learning. A culture of permission-giving and play grounded in discernment of the Spirit and trust in God can break open systems that were designed to standardize and control. Gatherings like church assemblies, pastor conferences, and other events can become spaces for spiritual practices, storytelling about experiments, "failures," and sharing discoveries.

Conclusion

The mixed ecology is messy, organic, and multi-layered. How it comes to life in a particular region or church system will look different depending on the context and circumstances. What helps keep it vital and functional is a shared sense of God's activity in creating and re-creating the church in our day. If we think of the church as a static thing that is up to us to sustain and save, we will fall into despair. When we lean into the energy and connections of the Holy Spirit, we are better able to adopt a posture of grace. Grace is the foundation of the church, after all—God's grace known to us in Christ. When we live in that grace it frees us to love one another and to hold each other with compassion rather than resentment, with abundance rather than scarcity and fear.

Traditional and emerging expressions of Christian community can work together in powerful ways. New forms of church meet people where they are in language and in ways they can understand. They can translate the tradition's treasures for new generations and teach the traditional church how to speak to those generations. Traditional churches offer wisdom and ways of worshiping and practicing the Christian faith that have been handed down over the centuries and unite us with all the faithful people who have gone before us. When they are connected, the energy flows in both directions. A thriving ecology has a diversity of species and a rich movement within it. It is a picture of abundant life.

Conclusion

> "As you, Father, are in me and I am in you, may they also be in us, so that the world may believe that you have sent me. The glory that you have given me I have given them, so that they may be one, as we are one, I in them and you in me, that they may become completely one, so that the world may know that you have sent me and have loved them even as you have loved me."
>
> —John 17:20-23

Just before he traveled across the Kidron Valley, slightly northeast of Jerusalem, to a garden where he was arrested, Jesus prayed for his disciples. In that prayer Jesus asked God that his apprentices and closest followers be protected, and that they be one as he and the Father are one. Jesus prays for this oneness not once, but twice. While he wants his joy "made complete" in them (17:13), the primary reason for this oneness is "so that the world may know that you have sent me" (17:23), and "so that the love with which you have loved me may be in them and I in them" (17:26).

The oneness Jesus desires for his followers is possible because it is present in God's very life. The Triune God is a community of love constituted by three persons in a profoundly mutual relationship—God the Father, God the Son (Jesus), and God the Holy Spirit. Each person of the Trinity is different and yet exists in mutual indwelling in which difference is embraced, not erased. The three persons of the Trinity work together to create, re-create, reconcile, heal, guide, comfort, and encourage.

Their shared life constitutes something larger than their distinct identities. Our participation in God's life through Christ and the Spirit means we too can experience oneness in Christ.

While the oneness Jesus prays for can feel challenging in our fragmented times, just remember the differences among the first disciples! They had different personalities, gifts, and aims, and some of them, like James and John (and their mother!), wanted to have more prestigious positions than their fellow disciples. Jesus's first disciples came from different places, trades, and walks of life. Together they grappled with who he was and they often fell short not only in their understanding, but in practicing Jesus's way of life. In Acts, we see very different expressions of the early Christian movement in places like Jerusalem and Antioch. We witness ethnic Jews wrestling with the thought of incorporating Gentiles into their movement. As the gospel spread across various countries and boundaries, Jesus's followers had to both contextualize the gospel and connect with the wider Jesus movement.

Christ has one church. This is the vision of the church's founder, Jesus. It is also ultimately the reality, despite the differences that divide Christians today. The early Christian movement wrestled with and incorporated cultural and contextual diversity into its life from the start. Its geographical spread prompted new missionary questions and forms of Christian community. The church has always been a dynamic phenomenon, reflecting the dynamism of God's Word and God's world. When it ceases to be so, it can be like the imperial Roman authorities Jesus and his fellow first-century Jews had to contend with, seeking to manage and exploit people under its control. Or it can adopt the narrow, exclusive hierarchies of Jesus's frequent opponents, the Pharisees and scribes.

Reform and renewal of the church today must start with Jesus and his way. We have an opportunity to learn more deeply how to live a Jesus-shaped life in whatever context we find ourselves: city, suburb, small town, rural, online, whatever culture or environment. We can recover the ancient spiritual practices, including prayer, that God uses to form us in Jesus's image. We can reflect more deeply on how Jesus's teachings speak to the spiritual hunger all around us—the despair, anxiety, fear, insecurities, divisions, and injustices that keep our neighbors up at night. We can be rooted in Jesus's life and love so we can show up as his followers in every space in our life—the spaces where we live, work, study, and play. We can love our neighbors in every one of these places by listening to them and attending to the Holy Spirit's invitation to share the one thing that can provide ultimate hope, healing, and transformation—a relationship with Jesus and the abundant life he offers.

In Western societies today, more and more of our neighbors have never been exposed to Jesus and his teachings. They've primarily heard or seen negative things about his followers, or the versions of Christ they've encountered are distorted. Church is not on their radar screens, and if they did come, it would in many cases feel foreign and insular. The work we believe the Holy Spirit is inviting Jesus's followers in the West into in this moment of history is humble, patient, and often small and unseen, just like a mustard seed. It's not work most of our inherited church systems were designed for.

We have been blessed to experience and meet Christian leaders working on the edges of their church systems in a variety of contexts. They are following the leadership of the Holy Spirit as they try small experiments to learn more about what God is up to in the lives of their neighbors. They are meeting neighbors where they are, as listeners and learners. Their lives have been changed by the gospel, and they want to share the joy and transformation they've experienced. We need to learn from these prophets, apostles, and evangelists who have trouble functioning in many of our current structures.

As part of his conversation with his disciples before his arrest, as recounted in John's Gospel, Jesus also offered a powerful organic metaphor:

> "I am the true vine, and my Father is the vinegrower. He removes every branch in me that bears no fruit. Every branch that bears fruit he prunes to make it bear more fruit. You have already been cleansed by the word that I have spoken to you. Abide in me as I abide in you. Just as the branch cannot bear fruit by itself unless it abides in the vine, neither can you unless you abide in me. I am the vine, you are the branches. Those who abide in me and I in them bear much fruit, because apart from me you can do nothing. Whoever does not abide in me is thrown away like a branch and withers; such branches are gathered, thrown into the fire, and burned. If you abide in me, and my words abide in you, ask for whatever you wish, and it will be done for you. My Father is glorified by this, that you bear much fruit and become

> my disciples. As the Father has loved me, so I have loved you; abide in my love. If you keep my commandments, you will abide in my love, just as I have kept my Father's commandments and abide in his love. I have said these things to you so that my joy may be in you, and that your joy may be complete." (John 15:1-11)

The church is one when it abides in the one true vine. This is a time of pruning for many churches. Notice that Jesus says branches that are bearing fruit are pruned alongside those that are not. The reality is that many church structures today are no longer bearing much spiritual fruit. Congregations that function primarily as clubs or social service agencies will not likely survive unless they learn to become communities where disciples of Jesus are formed and apprenticed. Fruit in this text is a direct outgrowth of abiding and being disciples.

Jesus implores his followers to be one as he and God are one. Instead of seeing other Christian groups as competitors, or worse, as enemies, how might we see them as God's fellow ambassadors, co-laborers in a larger vineyard, a mixed ecology? How might we learn from Christians from other traditions who excel in discipleship, justice work, and meeting neighbors where they are? What are we willing to give up in order to collaborate, share with, and learn from our brothers and sisters in Christ in various forms of church and Christian community today? Are we able to see the God-created humanity and dignity of Christians who have been formed by different cultural worlds? This can only begin with a posture of curiosity and openness.

The Holy Spirit is the Christian way of talking about God's power and presence in the here and now. It is the Holy Spirit who animates and energizes the church to join with neighbors in mission. We do not have to try to do this work on our own. If we do, we shall surely fail. Tapping into the energy and movement of the Holy Spirit involves prayerful listening, identifying where life-giving connections are emerging, paying attention to the margins of our communities, and tolerating the ambiguity of not having it all figured out ahead of time. The Spirit empowers all kinds of voices to speak, especially those who are socially marginalized (Joel 2:28-29). That is the kind of iterative, adventurous journey we see in the Book of Acts, for instance, where ordinary people are empowered for extraordinary things under the Spirit's leadership.

What's at Stake

In our work with churches and their leaders over the years, we have seen a mixture of motivations for engaging the work of adaptation and innovation. Sometimes, it comes from fear of losing beloved institutions that have shaped lives over generations. Other times, it arises from anxieties about livelihoods for those of us who make our livings within church structures. Sometimes there is a competitive spirit of achievement at play. Other times it is about tackling the challenge of institutional renewal for its own sake—like turning around a failing business. These are all understandable reasons to take up the challenge of changing how we do church. But they are insufficient.

God has a church in the world to bear God's power to heal, forgive, reconcile, restore, and unite people in Christ in the power of the Spirit. The church is a community that embodies and enacts encounters with the risen Christ, the one in whom we see and know what true human life—abundant life—looks and feels like. In a culture that says we're on our own to save ourselves, the church confesses God's ultimate power to deliver us from all that divides and destroys human life. In a society fractured along social and cultural lines, the church is a community in which God brings together people from every tribe and nation, breaking down the dividing walls of hostility. In a country and world full of idolatrous stories and leaders who claim to be saviors, the church practices the politics of an alternative reign or kingdom.

The disconnect between this list and what is evident in many institutional expressions of church is why so many neighbors don't trust the church and have no interest in joining its present forms. This is where the deep underlying challenge of learning to follow Jesus and live his way in a culture resistant to the gospel must be our central focus. It is only as we ourselves encounter Jesus in one another and learn how to practice and share an alternative way of life together that we will have something to offer our neighbors. The Christian life is about humility, simplicity, and relationships, which is how Jesus came in the first place.

As we live more deeply in the power of the Spirit into Jesus's story, we are led to join our neighbors in their suffering, loss, insecurity, fear, and struggle. Contemporary Western culture is a culture of individual striving and achievement; no wonder people are so lonely and burned out.[1] Even those who are "successfully" playing the game are haunted by the prospect that they aren't enough. Rather than waiting for people to come into our inherited structures to encounter God's promises, the church in our time is being called to venture incarnationally into neighborhood spaces where life plays out, listening, loving, and standing compassionately with people amidst the fissures, ruptures, and lies of our culture's narratives.

Joining up with what the Holy Spirit is already up to in our neighborhoods happens best when we recognize all the gifts the church has to offer in its different forms. Not everyone will be ready to take this journey at the same time. Time-honored congregations can be bases from which small teams of explorers set out and return with stories and learnings. Every form of church has a role to play, and the more we create space for different expressions of church that reach the diversity of people in today's world, the more the church as a whole will flourish. Jesus's vineyard has many different branches. Rooted in the same vine, we can all bear fruit.

Notes

Introduction

1. We use the phrase "global majority" in this book to refer to people from the Global South and Global South heritage.

2. Dwight's earlier books *People of the Way* and *The Agile Church* explore this congregation and some of the initiatives more fully.

3. Lesslie Newbigin, *The Open Secret: An Introduction to the Theology of Mission* (Grand Rapids, MI: Eerdmans, 1978), 124.

4. See Amanda Ripley, *High Conflict: Why We Get Trapped and How Get Out* (New York: Simon and Schuster, 2022).

5. See Josh Packard and Ashleigh Hope, *Church Refugees* (Loveland, CO: Group Publishing, 2015) and Jim Davis and Michael Graham, *The Great Dechurching* (Grand Rapids, MI: Zondervan, 2023).

6. Former Archbishop of Canterbury Rowan Williams began using the phrase "mixed economy" of church while serving as a bishop in Wales. This has been reframed in subsequent discourse in the UK to "mixed ecology," which better reflects the organic metaphors of scripture.

7. Stuart Murray, *A Vast Minority: Church and Mission in a Plural Culture* (London: Paternoster, 2015), ix.

8. Bishop Thorpe regularly uses this statement in his public speaking; he confirmed it through private correspondence with the authors.

9. Peter J. Denning and Robert Dunham, *The Innovator's Way* (Cambridge, MA: MIT Press, 2012), 6.

10. Steve Aisthorpe, *Rewilding the Church* (Edinburgh: Saint Andrew Press, 2020), 2.

11. Ibid., 74.

12. See Tom Holland, *Dominion: How the Christian Revolution Remade the World* (New York: Basic Books, 2019).

13. See Stuart Murray, *Post-Christendom: Church and Mission in a Strange New World* (Waynesboro, GA: Paternoster, 2004). For an exploration of this history in the United States and the Episcopal Church specifically, see Stephanie Spellers, *The Church Cracked Open* (New York: Church Publishing, 2021).

14. See Stefan Paas, *Church Planting in the Secular West: Learning from the European Experience* (Grand Rapids, MI: W.B. Eerdmans, 2016), 101-102. See also his book *Pilgrims and Priests: Christian Mission in a Post-Christian Society* (London: SCM Press, 2019).

15. Stuart Murray, *A Vast Minority: Church and Mission in a Plural Culture* (London: Paternoster, 2015), 72.

16. See Tim Alberta, *The Kingdom, the Power, and the Glory* (New York: Harper, 2024).

17. Paas, *Church Planting in the Secular West*, 100-101.

18. See Jehu J. Hanciles, *Beyond Christendom: Globalization, African Migration, and the Transformation of the West* (Maryknoll, NY: Orbis, 2008).

19. Harvey Kwiyani, *Sent Forth: African Missionary Work in the West* (Maryknoll, NY: Orbis, 2014), 28.

20. Peter Vethanayagamony, "Mission from the Rest to the West: The Changing Landscape of World Christianity and Global Mission" in Obgu U. Kalo, Peter Vethanayagamony and Edmond Kee-Fook Chia, eds., *Mission After Christendom: Emergent Themes in Contemporary Mission* (Louisville, KY: Westminster/John Knox Press, 2010), 69.

21. See Samuel Wells, *Incarnational Ministry: Being with the Church* (Grand Rapids, MI: Eerdmans, 2017).

22. Hanciles, *Beyond Christendom*, 265.

Chapter 1: A Time of Disconnection

1. We are drawing here on Charles Taylor, *A Secular Age* (Cambridge, MA: Belknap Press, 2007), among other sources for this summary.

2. This view was famously articulated by John Locke in "A Letter Concerning Toleration." See Maurice Cranston, ed., *Locke on Politics, Religion, and Education* (New York: Collier, 1965).

3. See Andrew Root, *Faith Formation in a Secular Age* (Grand Rapids, MI: Baker Academic, 2017), 63-72.

4. Taylor, *A Secular Age*, 473-504.

5. Jeffrey Mahan, *Church as Network: Christian Life and Connection in Digital Culture* (Lanham, MD: Rowman and Littlefield, 2021), 51.

6. Ibid., 41.

7. See Ulrich Beck and Elisabeth Beck-Gernsheim, *Individualization* (Thousand Oaks, CA: Sage, 2002).

8. Ted Smith, *The End of Theological Education* (Grand Rapids, MI: Eerdmans, 2023), 105.

9. Ibid.

10. Yuval Levin, *A Time to Build* (New York: Basic Books, 2020), 48-49.

11. See Adam Seligman, *Modernity's Wager* (Princeton: Princeton U.P., 2000). See also Mark Lau Branson and Alan J. Roxburgh, *Leadership, God's Agency and Disruptions: Confronting Modernity's Wager* (Eugene, OR; Cascade Books, 2020).

12. See Pat Taylor Ellison and Patrick R. Keifert, *Dwelling in the Word* (St. Paul, MN: Church Innovations Institute, 2011) or https://faithlead.org/blog/how-to-lead-dwelling-in-the-word/.

13. For more details on these practices, see Faith+Lead, *Faithful Innovation Leader Companion* (St. Paul, MN: Luther Seminary, 2022) or www.faithlead.org.

14. See Dwight J. Zscheile, Michael Binder, and Tessa Pinkstaff, *Leading Faithful Innovation: Following God into a Hopeful Future* (Minneapolis: Fortress Press, 2023).

15. Greg L. Hawkins and Cally Parkinson, *Reveal: Where Are You?* (Barrington, IL: Willow Creek Resources, 2007).

16. See https://renewalworks.org/researchsummary/.

17. John Mark Comer, *Practicing the Way: Be with Jesus, Become like Him, Do as He Did* (Colorado Springs, CO: Waterbrook, 2024), 11.

18. Eun K. Strawser, *Centering Discipleship* (Downers Grove, IL: InterVarsity Press, 2023).

19. See Smith, *The End of Theological Education*.

20. Cited in G. Jeffrey MacDonald, *Part-Time is Plenty: Thriving Without Full-Time Clergy* (Louisville: Westminster/John Knox, 2020). 19.

21. Cited in Ted A. Smith, *The End of Theological Education*, 107. ELCA statistics are from March 2016.

22. Ibid.

23. Catherine Neelly Burton, "The Future of the PC(USA) Is Pastor-Less, and That's OK." *Presbyterian Outlook*, January 2024.

Chapter 2: Rediscovering Roots

1. See Albert Raboteau, *Slave Religion: The 'Invisible Institution' in the Antebellum South* (New York: Oxford U.P., 1978). See also Alexia Salvatierra and Brandon Wrencher, *Buried Seeds: Learning from the Vibrant Resistance of Marginalized Christian Communities* (Grand Rapids, MI: Baker Academic, 2022).

2. The Message translation.

3. Lesslie Newbigin, *The Open Secret*, rev. ed. (Grand Rapids, MI: Eerdmans, 1995). 32.

4. Andrew Walls, *The Missionary Movement in Christian History* (Maryknoll, NY: Orbis, 1996), 26-28.

5. Lesslie Newbigin, *Foolishness to the Greeks* (Grand Rapids, MI: Eerdmans, 1986), 4.

6. Walls, *Missionary Movement in Christian History*. See also Lamin Sanneh, *Translating the Message: The Missionary Impact on Culture* (Maryknoll, NY: Orbis Books, 1989).

7. Newbign, *The Open Secret*, 19-20.

8. Lesslie Newbigin, "Can the West Be Converted?," *International Bulletin of Missionary Research* 11, no. 1 (January 1987), 2-7.

9. Lesslie Newbigin, *Living Hope in a Changing World* (London: Alpha International Holy Trinity Brompton, 2003), 83. Cited in Michael Goheen and Timothy M. Sheridan, *Becoming a Missionary Church: Lesslie Newbigin and Contemporary Church Movements* (Grand Rapids, MI: Baker Academic, 2022), 69.

10. Goheen and Sheridan, *Becoming a Missionary Church*, 69.

11. Ibid., 70.

12. William Cavanaugh, *The Uses of Idolatry* (New York: Oxford University Press, 2024), 1.

13. Ibid., 51.

14. Ibid., 83.

15. Lesslie Newbigin, "Biblical Authority," Newbigin Archives, University of Birmingham (unpublished article, 1997), 2. Cited in Goheen and Sheridan, *Becoming a Missionary Church*, 74.

16. Goheen and Sheridan, *Becoming a Missionary Church*, 157.

17. Cavanaugh, *Uses of Idolatry*, 5.

18. See Martyn Snow with Lusa Nsenga-Ngoy, Saju Muthalaly, Jessie Tang and Florence Gildea, *An Intercultural Church for an Intercultural World: Reflections on Gift Exchange* (London: Church House Publishing, 2024).

19. Jehu J. Hanciles, *Beyond Christendom: Globalization, African Migration, and the Transformation of the West* (Maryknoll, NY: Orbis, 2008), 363.

20. See James Burtchaell, *From Synagogue to Church: Public Services and Offices in the Earliest Christian Communities* (Cambridge: Cambridge University Press, 1992).

21. Craig Ott and Gene Wilson, *Global Church Planting: Biblical Principles and Best Practices for Multiplication* (Grand Rapids, MI: Baker Academic, 2011), 110.

22. Jennifer Wojciechowski, *Women in the Christian Story* (Minneapolis: Fortress Press, 2022), 83-84.

23. Philip Harrold, "Contextual Churches in History" in Michael Moynagh, *Church for Every Context* (London: SCM Press, 2012), 39.

24. Ibid, 43-44.

25. See Alexia Salvatierra and Brandon Wrencher, *Buried Seeds: Learning from the Vibrant Resistance of Marginalized Christian Communities* (Grand Rapids, MI: Baker Academic, 2022), 11-28.

26. "What Is the House Church?"The Center for House Church Theology, https://housechurchtheology.com/what-is-the-house-church, accessed March 1, 2024.

27. Harvey Kwiyani, *Sent Forth: African Missionary Work in the West* (Maryknoll, NY: Orbis, 2014), 59.

Chapter 3: Church Planting

1. See Edgar Schein, *Organizational Culture and Leadership*, 3rd ed. (San Francisco: Jossey-Bass, 2004).

2. Mark Lau Branson and Nicholas Warnes, eds. S*tarting Missional Churches: Life with God in the Neighborhood* (Downers Grove, IL: IVP, 2014), 14-27.

3. Tim Keller, *Center Church: Doing Balanced, Gospel-Centered Ministry in Your City* (Grand Rapids, MI: Zondervan, 2012), 356.

4. Nicholas Warnes, *Deconstructing Church Planting* (Los Angeles: Cyclical Publishing, 2021).

5. Stuart Murray, *Planting Churches in the 21st Century* (Scottdale, PA: Herald Press, 2010), 14.

6. Ed Stetzer, *Planting Missional Churches* (Nashville: Broadman & Holman, 2006), 156.

7. Fiona Mayne, "Haywood Village Church, Weston-super-Mare" in John McGinley, ed., *Send Me: Stories of Ordinary People Planting New Churches* (London: Gregory Centre for Church Multiplication, 2022), 5-11.

8. Ibid., 8.

9. See https://gasstreet.church/storysofar, accessed April 25, 2024 and Ric Thorpe, *Resource Churches* (London: Gregory Centre for Church Multiplication, 2021), 27.

10. See Keller, *Center Church*, 356.

11. Ric Thorpe, *Resource Churches*, 1.

12. Ibid., 24.

13. https://newcitychurchla.com/about/our-history/, accessed May 1, 2024. See also Kevin Haah, "A Beautiful Community of Diversity: New City Church" in Branson and Warnes, eds., *Starting Missional Churches*.

14. "New City Profile 2019," https://newcitychurchla.com/wp-content/uploads/2020/02/FAMILY-PROFILE-2019-1.pdf, accessed May 1, 2024.

15. Stetzer, *Planting Missional Churches,* 109.

16. Murray, *Planting Churches in the 21st Century*, 126-30.

17. See George Lings, *The Day of Small Things* (Sheffield: Church Army Research Unit, 2016), 89. This echoes observations made about church planting in other contexts as well.

Chapter 4: Fresh Expressions

1. https://freshexpressions.org.uk/, accessed March 9, 2024.

2. George Lings, *The Day of Small Things: An Analysis of Fresh Expressions of Church in 21 Dioceses in the Church of England* (Sheffield: Church Army Research Unit, 2016), 18.

3. Michael Moynagh, *Church for Every Context* (London: SCM Press, 2012), 99.

4. Lings, *Day of Small Things*, 40.

5. Michael Moynagh, *Being Church, Doing Life* (Oxford: Monarch Books, 2014), 41.

6. Ibid., 55-56.

7. Michael Moynagh, *Church in Life* (Eugene, OR: Cascade Books, 2018), 152.

8. David McCarthy, *Seeing Afresh: Learning from Fresh Expressions of Church* (Edinburgh: St. Andrew Press, 2019), 15-16. See also Moynagh, *Being Church, Doing Life*, 31 and https://www.hotchocolate.org.uk/, accessed May 8, 2024.

9. Moynagh, *Being Church, Doing Life*, 126.

10. Archbishop's Council on Mission and Public Affairs, *Mission-Shaped Church* (London: Church House, 2004), 99.

11. Moynagh, *Church in Life*, 242.

12. Ibid, 248.

13. https://messychurchusa.org/global-messy-church-movement/, accessed May 15, 2024.

14. Lings, *Day of Small Things*, 10, 62.

15. Church of England's Ministry Council, 2016.

16. Moynagh, *Church in Life*, 310-12.

17. Eido Research and the Church of England, *Fresh Expressions of Church: Fruitfulness Framework Report*, 2021.

18. Moynagh, *Church in Life*, 141.

19. Michael Moynagh, comment in private conversation with author.

20. Ibid, 191.

21. Lings, *The Day of Small Things*, 11.

22. He shared these observations in a private conversation with the authors in January 2024.

Chapter 5: Megachurches and Microchurches

1. https://outreach100.com/churches/lutheran-church-of-hope, accessed May 23, 2024.

2. Ted Smith, *The End of Theological Education* (Grand Rapids, MI: Eerdmans, 2023), 102.

3. Scott Thumma and Dave Travis, *Beyond Megachurch Myths* (San Francisco: Jossey-Bass, 2007), 5.

4. Ibid., xviii.

5. Warren Bird and Scott Thumma, *Megachurch 2020: The Changing Reality in America's Largest Churches* (Hartford, CT: Hartford Institute for Religion Research, 2020), 2.

6. Thumma and Travis, *Beyond Megachurch Myths*, 28.

7. Bird and Thumma, *Megachurch 2020*, 4.

8. Thumma and Travis, *Beyond Megachurch Myths*, 139.

9. Bird and Thumma, *Megachurch 2020*, 11.

10. Thumma and Travis, *Beyond Megachurch Myths*, 22.

11. Ibid, 216.

12. Thumma and Travis, *Beyond Megachurch Myths*, 15.

13. Ibid, 81.

14. Ibid., 46-47.

15. James K. Wellman Jr., Katie E. Corcoran, and Kate J. Stockly, *High on God: How Megachurches Won the Heart of America* (New York: Oxford U.P., 2020), 193. See also Thumma and Travis, *Beyond Megachurch Myths*, 58.

16. See Kate Bowler, *Blessed: A History of the American Prosperity Gospel* (New York: Oxford University Press, 2013).

17. See Tim Alberta, *The Kingdom, the Power and the Glory* (New York: HarperCollins, 2023), 106-24.

18. Bird and Thumma, *Megachurch 2020*, 12.

19. Taylor McCall and Hugh Halter, *Brave Cities* (Richmond, VA: 100 Movements Publishing, 2024).

20. Ibid., 168.

21. Brian Sanders, *Underground Church* (Grand Rapids: Zondervan, 2018), 34.

22. Ibid., 60-66.

23. See https://discoverybiblestudy.org/

24. Brian Sanders, *Microchurches (A Smaller Way)* (Tampa, FL: Underground Media, 2022), 3.

25. Ibid., 13

26. Ibid., 27.

27. Tampa Underground (https://www.tampaunderground.com/) and KC Underground (based in Kansas City; https://kcunderground.org/) are two prominent microchurch network organizations.

28. Sanders, *Underground Church*, 198.

29. McCall and Halter, *Brave Cities*, 88.

Chapter 6: Digital Church

1. Life Church Financial Statement, https://cms-assets.life.church/lc-site/pages/give/Financial%20Statements/2024/Web_Financials_09-24.pdf

2. Keith Anderson, *The Digital Cathedral: Networked Ministry in a Wireless World* (New York: Morehouse, 2015), 83.

3. See Deanna Thompson, *The Virtual Body of Christ in a Suffering World* (Nashville: Abingdon Press, 2016), 58-59.

4. Jeffrey Mahan, *Church as Network: Christian Life and Connection in Digital Culture* (Lanham, MD: Rowman and Littlefield, 2021), 41-44.

5. Ibid., 45-46.

6. Ibid., 46-49.

7. Anderson, *Digital Cathedral*, 163.

8. Ibid.

9. Ibid., 17-21.

10. Anderson, *Digital Cathedral*, 91.

11. Michael Frost, *Incarnate: The Body of Christ in an Age of Disengagement* (Downers Grove, IL: IVP Books, 2014).

Chapter 7: The Mixed Ecology: A Contemporary Case Study

1. Office of National Statistics (UK), "Religion, England and Wales, 2021," https://www.ons.gov.uk/peoplepopulationandcommunity/culturalidentity/religion/bulletins/religionenglandandwales/census2021, accessed March 6, 2024.

2. Ken Eames, *Statistics for Mission 2022* (London: Church of England Data Services, 2023), 5.

3. Stuart Murray, *A Vast Minority: Church and Mission in a Plural Culture* (London: Paternoster, 2015).

4. George Lings, "A History of Fresh Expressions and Church Planting in the Church of England" in David Goodhew, ed., *Church Growth in Britain: 1980 to the Present* (Burlington, VT: Ashgate, 2012), 164-65.

5. Cited in Archbishop's Council on Mission and Public Affairs, *Mission-Shaped Church* (London: Church House, 2004), 19.

6. See Manuel Castells, *The Rise of the Network Society* (Malden, MA: Blackwells, 2000).

7. *Mission-Shaped Church*, 12.

8. Ibid, xi.

9. Lings, "A History of Fresh Expressions and Church Planting in the Church of England," 161.

10. https://www.churchofengland.org/, accessed March 8, 2024.

11. Lings, 165.

12. *Mission-Shaped Church*, 32.

13. John Wolffe and Bob Jackson, "Anglican Resurgence: The Church of England in London" in David Goodhew, ed., *Church Growth in Britain: 1980 to the Present* (Burlington, VT: Ashgate, 2012), 35.

14. Steve Taylor, *First Expressions: Innovation and the Mission of God* (London: SCM Press, 2019), 62-63.

15. See http://freshworship.org/about/whathappens.html, accessed March 9, 2024.

16. *The Engine Room Five Year Report*, https://engineroom.org.uk/five-year-report/, accessed July 17, 2024.

17. In the UK, the phrase "fresh expressions" is now increasingly being replaced by "new worshiping communities," though it still functions there and in other global contexts.

18. https://freshexpressions.org.uk/, accessed March 9, 2024.

19. *Mission-Shaped Church*, 34.

20. Michael Moynagh, *Church in Life* (Eugene, OR: Cascade, 2018).

21. *Mission-Shaped Church*.

22. George Lings, *The Day of Small Things: An Analysis of Fresh Expressions in 21 Dioceses of the Church of England* (Sheffield: Church Army, 2016), 10.

23. *Mission-Shaped Church*, v.

24. *Mission-Shaped Church*, 84-94.

25. *Mission-Shaped Church*, 99.

26. Michael Moynagh, *Church for Every Context* (London: SCM Press, 2012), 67.

27. See, for example, Andrew Davison and Alison Milbank, *For the Parish* (London: SCM Press, 2010).

28. Taylor, 109-24.

29. Within the UK, the term "pioneer" is used to describe "People called by God who are the first to see and creatively respond to the Holy Spirit's initiatives with those outside the church; gathering others around them as they seek to establish a new contextual Christian community."

30. https://ccx.org.uk.

31. Church of England, "Qualities for Formation Ordained IME1 Pioneer," https://www.churchofengland.org/sites/default/files/2021-11/ime-1-priest-pioneer-qualities-and-evidence-from-autumn-2022.pdf.

32. See Christian Selvaratnam, *The Craft of Church Planting: Exploring the Lost Wisdom of Apprenticeship* (London: SCM Press, 2022).

33. Church of England Vision and Strategy, https://www.churchofengland.org/about/vision-and-strategy, accessed March 10, 2024.

34. Ibid.

35. See Pew Research Center, *Religious "Nones" in America: Who They Are and What They Believe* (Pew Research Center, January 2024).

36. See Goodhew, ed., *Church Growth in Britain.*

37. See Chigor Chike, *African Christianity in Britain: Diaspora, Doctrines, and Dialogue* (Bloomington, IN: AuthorHouse, 2007) and Harvey C. Kwiyani, *Sent Forth: African Missionary Work in the West* (Maryknoll, NY: Orbis, 2014).

38. Moynagh, *Church for Every Context*, 81.

39. We are indebted to Michael Moynagh for these observations shared in personal communication with the authors.

Chapter 8: Making Space, Learning, and Leading Together

1. See https://www.lightwave.community/about-lightwave, accessed July 22, 2024.

2. https://ccx.org.uk/myriad-lay-led-planting/

3. John Kotter, *Accelerate* (Boston: Harvard Business Review Press, 2014), vii-viii.

4. Sally Gaze, personal correspondence with the authors.

5. See https://www.stpetersbethnalgreen.org/, accessed July 24, 2024.

6. Ed Olsworth-Peter, *Mixed Ecology: Inhabiting an Integrated Church* (London: SPCK, 2024), 70-72.

7. See ibid., 59-60.

8. For instance, Luther Seminary's Faith+Lead (www.faithlead.org) provides on-demand courses, learning communities, workshops, coaching, and training, as does Fresh Expressions North America (www.freshexpressions.com) and a variety of other training organizations, such as the V3 Movement (www.thev3movement.org) and Cyclical (www.cyclicalinc.com). Many denominations also have equipping networks.

9. www.faithlead.org

Conclusion

1. See Byung-Chul Han, *The Burnout Society* (Stanford, CA: Stanford University Press, 2015), 10.

For Further Reading

Aisthorpe, Steve. *Rewilding the Church.* Edinburgh: Saint Andrew Press, 2020.

Anderson, Keith. *The Digital Cathedral: Networked Ministry in a Wireless World.* New York: Morehouse, 2015.

Archbishop's Council on Mission and Public Affairs, *Mission-Shaped Church.* London: Church House Publishing, 2004.

Beck, Michael Adam and Jorge Acevedo. *A Field Guide to Methodist Fresh Expressions.* Nashville: Abingdon Press, 2020.

Bird, Warren and Scott Thumma. *Megachurch 2020: The Changing Reality in America's Largest Churches.* Hartford, CT: Hartford Institute for Religion Research, 2020.

Branson, Mark Lau and Alan J. Roxburgh, *Leadership, God's Agency and Disruptions: Confronting Modernity's Wager.* Eugene, OR; Cascade Books, 2020.

Branson, Mark Lau and Juan F. Martinez. *Churches, Cultures and Leadership*, second ed. Downers Grove, IL: InterVarsity Press, 2023.

Branson, Mark Lau and Nicholas Warnes, eds. *Starting Missional Churches: Life with God in the Neighborhood.* Downers Grove, IL: InterVarsity Press, 2014.

Cavanaugh, William. *The Uses of Idolatry.* New York: Oxford University Press, 2024.

Comer, John Mark. *Practicing the Way: Be with Jesus, Become like Him, Do as He Did.* Colorado Springs, CO: Waterbrook, 2024.

Dunlop, Andrew. *Out of Nothing: A Cross-Shaped Approach to Fresh Expressions.* London: SCM Press, 2018.

Fout, Jason A. *Learning from London.* Cincinnati, OH: Forward Movement, 2019.

Gaze, Sally. *Mission-Shaped and Rural.* London: Church House Publishing, 2011.

Goheen, Michael. *The Church and Its Vocation: Lesslie Newbigin's Missionary Ecclesiology.* Grand Rapids, MI: Baker Academic, 2018.

Han, Byung-Chul. *The Burnout Society.* Stanford, CA: Stanford University Press, 2015.

Hanciles, Jehu J. *Beyond Christendom: Globalization, African Migration, and the Transformation of the West.* Maryknoll, NY: Orbis, 2008.

Hope, Susan. *Mission-Shaped Spirituality.* New York: Seabury Books, 2010.

Keller, Tim. *Center Church: Doing Balanced, Gospel-Centered Ministry in Your City.* Grand Rapids, MI: Zondervan, 2012.

Kwiyani, Harvey. *Sent Forth: African Missionary Work in the West.* Maryknoll, NY: Orbis, 2014.

Lings, George. *The Day of Small Things: An Analysis of Fresh Expressions in 21 Dioceses of the Church of England.* Sheffield: Church Army, 2016.

MacDonald, Jeffrey. *Part-Time is Plenty: Thriving Without Full-Time Clergy.* Louisville: Westminster/John Knox, 2020.

McCall, Taylor and Hugh Halter. *Brave Cities.* Richmond, VA: 100 Movements Publishing, 2024.

McGinley, John ed. *Send Me: Stories of Ordinary People Planting New Churches.* London: Gregory Centre for Church Multiplication, 2022.

Moynagh, Michael. *Being Church, Doing Life.* Grand Rapids, MI: Monarch Books, 2014.

____. *Church for Every Context.* London: SCM Press, 2012.

____. *Church in Life.* Eugene, OR: Cascade, 2018.

____. *Giving the Church.* London: SCM Press, 2024.

Murray, Stuart. *A Vast Minority: Church and Mission in a Plural Culture.* London: Paternoster, 2015.

Newbigin, Lesslie. *Foolishness to the Greeks.* Grand Rapids, MI: Eerdmans, 1986.

____. *The Open Secret: An Introduction to the Theology of Mission.* Grand Rapids, MI: Eerdmans, 1978.

Olsworth-Peter, Ed. *Mixed Ecology: Inhabiting an Integrated Church.* London: SPCK, 2024.

Ott, Craig and Gene Wilson. *Global Church Planting: Biblical Principles and Best Practices for Multiplication.* Grand Rapids, MI: Baker Academic, 2011.

Paas, Stefan. *Church Planting in the Secular West: Learning from the European Experience.* Grand Rapids, MI: W.B. Eerdmans, 2016.

____. *Pilgrims and Priests: Christian Mission in a Post-Christian Society.* London: SCM Press, 2019.

Packard, Josh and Ashleigh Hope. *Church Refugees.* Loveland, CO: Group Publishing, 2015.

Salvatierra, Alexia and Brandon Wrencher. *Buried Seeds: Learning from the Vibrant Resistance of Marginalized Christian Communities.* Grand Rapids, MI: Baker Academic, 2022.

Sanders, Brian. *Microchurches (A Smaller Way).* Tampa, FL: Underground Media, 2022.

____. *Underground Church.* Grand Rapids, MI: Zondervan, 2018.

Selvaratnam, Christian. *The Craft of Church Planting: Exploring the Lost Wisdom of Apprenticeship.* London: SCM Press, 2022.

Smith, Ted. *The End of Theological Education.* Grand Rapids, MI: Eerdmans, 2023.

Snow, Martyn with Lusa Nsenga-Ngoy, Saju Muthalaly, Jessie Tang and Florence Gildea. *An Intercultural Church for an Intercultural World: Reflections on Gift Exchange.* London: Church House Publishing, 2024.

Solomon, Yolanda. *Discipleship as Holy Collaboration: Helping Others Follow Jesus in Real Life*. Downers Grove, IL: InterVarsity Press, 2024.

Spellers, Stephanie. *The Church Cracked Open: Disruption, Decline, and New Hope for Beloved Community*. New York: Church Publishing, 2021.

Stetzer, Ed. *Planting Missional Churches*. Nashville: Broadman & Holman, 2006.

Strawser, Eun K. *Centering Discipleship*. Downers Grove, IL: InterVarsity Press, 2023.

Taylor, Steve. *First Expressions: Innovation and the Mission of God*. London: SCM Press, 2019.

Thompson, Deanna. *The Virtual Body of Christ in a Suffering World*. Nashville: Abingdon Press, 2016.

Thorpe, Ric. *Resource Churches*. London: Gregory Centre for Church Multiplication, 2021.

Thumma, Scott and Dave Travis. *Beyond Megachurch Myths*. San Francisco: Jossey-Bass, 2007.

Tizon, Al. *Whole and Reconciled: Gospel, Church, and Mission in a Fractured World*. Grand Rapids, MI: Baker Academic, 2018.

Vethanayagamony, Peter. "Mission from the Rest to the West: The Changing Landscape of World Christianity and Global Mission" in Obgu U. Kalo, Peter Vethanayagamony and Edmond Kee-Fook Chia, eds., *Mission After Christendom: Emergent Themes in Contemporary Mission*. Louisville, KY: Westminster/John Knox Press, 2010, 59-70.

Wellman, James K., Katie E. Corcoran, and Kate J. Stockly, *High on God: How Megachurches Won the Heart of America*. New York: Oxford U.P., 2021.

Wells, Samuel. *Incarnational Ministry: Being with the Church*. Grand Rapids, MI: Eerdmans, 2017.

Wojciechowski, Jennifer. *Women in the Christian Story.* Minneapolis: Fortress Press, 2022.

Zscheile, Dwight J. *The Agile Church: Spirit-Led Innovation in an Uncertain Age.* Harrisburg, PA: Morehouse, 2014.

Zscheile, Dwight J., Michael Binder, and Tessa Pinkstaff, *Leading Faithful Innovation: Following God into a Hopeful Future.* Minneapolis: Fortress Press, 2023.